What readers are saying about *Pragmatic Version Control Using Git*

Pragmatic Version Control Using Git is an excellent guide to getting you started with Git. It will teach you not only how to get yourself started but also how to cooperate with others and how to keep your history clean.

► **Pieter de Bie**
Author, GitX

If you are thinking of using Git, I highly recommend this book. If you are not using a version control system (and code or create content on a computer), put the book down, slap yourself, pick the book back up, and buy it.

► **Jacob Taylor**
Entrepreneur and Cofounder, SugarCRM Inc.

Not only has this book convinced me that Git has something to offer over CVS and Subversion, but it has also showed me how I can benefit from using it myself even if I'm using it alone in a CVS/Subversion environment. I expect to be a full-time Git user soon after reading this, which is hard to believe considering this is the first distributed version control system I've ever looked at.

► **Chuck Burgess**
2008 PEAR Group Member

Travis has done an excellent job taking a tricky subject and making it accessible, useful, and relevant. You'll find distributed version control and Git much less mysterious after reading this book.

► **Mike Mason**
Author, *Pragmatic Version Control Using Subversion*

Pragmatic Version Control

Using Git

Pragmatic Version Control

Using Git

Travis Swicegood

The Pragmatic Bookshelf
Raleigh, North Carolina Dallas, Texas

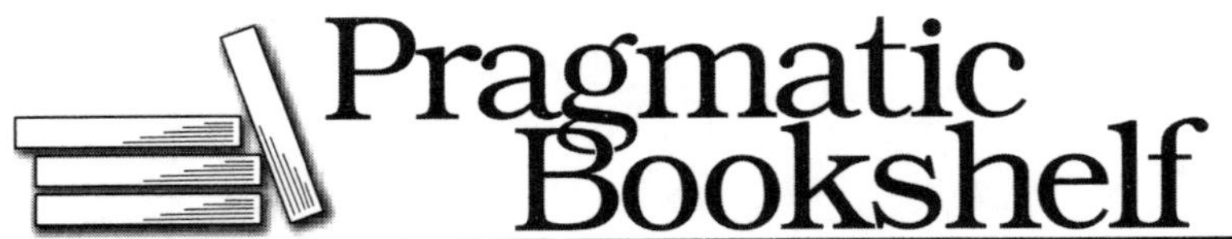

Our Pragmatic courses, workshops, and other products can help you and your team create better software and have more fun. For more information, as well as the latest Pragmatic titles, please visit us at

http://www.pragprog.com

Printed in the United States of America.

ISBN-10: 1-934356-15-8

ISBN-13: 978-1-934356-15-9

Printed on acid-free paper.

P2.0 printing, March 2009

Version: 2009-3-8

Contents

Acknowledgments

Although my name is on this book as the author, it is only here because of a long list of people. Please indulge me while I take a moment to thank them.

Thanks to Dave Thomas and Andy Hunt for taking the chance on a new author. The entire team they've put together at Pragmatic Bookshelf is amazing. I owe a special thanks to my editor, the ever helpful Susannah Davidson Pfalzer.

I would also like to thank all of those who offered me feedback on the book as it progressed through beta form. Especially helpful was the great team of technical reviewers: Chuck Burgess, Pieter de Bie, Stuart Halloway, Junio Hamano, Chris Hartjes, Mike Mason, John Mertic, Gary Sherman, Jacob Taylor, and Tommi "Tv" Virtanen. Thanks also to the wonderful teams of developers and colleagues at SugarCRM and Ning who supported me while I wrote this book.

Finally, I would like to thank my friends and family for their support and understanding while I wrote this book. My wonderful wife, Meg, put up with the late nights and "work weekends" with very little complaining. Without her support, and that from the rest of my friends and family, this book wouldn't be here today.

Preface

Development teams around the globe are changing. They are dropping their clunky, old, *centralized* version control systems (VCSs) in favor of Git, which is a lightweight, distributed version control system (DVCS) and relative newcomer to the version control world.

First here's a quick overview: a version control system is like a bank vault. You take your valuables—in our case as developers, these valuables are the source code we write—and deposit them in the bank for safekeeping.[1] Each change you mark—or *commit*—is recorded, and you can go back over the history just like you can review your bank statement.

In the Git world, it's like you walk around with your own vault that has an automated teller attached right to it. You can fully disconnect from everyone else, share what you want, and of course keep track of your project's history. The brainchild of Linus Torvalds, Git was originally developed to track changes made to the Linux kernel. Git has matured from the original rough collection of scripts Linus created in a few weeks into a rich toolkit. Its following strengths can help you as a programmer:

- *Distributed architecture*: Disconnect completely, and work without the distractions of an always-on Internet connection.

- *Easy branching and merging*: Creating branches is easy, cheap, and fast, and unlike some version control systems, merging everything back together—even multiple times—is a snap.

1. As I write this, we're in the middle of a $700 billion bailout of the American banking system, so maybe a bank isn't the best of analogies. Don't think about that part; just think of banks the way they're *supposed* to work.

- *Subversion communication*: Are you the only one in your company ready to make the switch? No worries if everyone else is still using Subversion. Git can import all your history from and send your changes back to a Subversion repository.

That's the sixty-second introduction to Git, and the rest of this book will build on this simple foundation.

Who's This Book For?

This book has something in it for everyone. If you're new to version control and the preceding paragraphs are all you know about it, this book will walk you through the basics and get you up to speed on how Git can help you.

If you're a seasoned developer and have a firm grasp on Subversion or CVS, you can skim Part I about Git specifics and jump into Part II to get into the good stuff—the Git commands and how they work.

What's in This Book?

This book is divided into four parts:

- Part I is an introduction to version control with a Git slant. Chapter 1, *Version Control the Git Way*, on page 3 is where you'll learn about version control in general and some of the fundamental concepts around VCS and how DVCS is different.

  Chapter 2, *Setting Up Git*, on page 15 walks you through installing and configuring Git, and Chapter 3, *Creating Your First Project*, on page 25 gets your feet wet by working on a simple HTML project[2] that showcases a lot of Git's functionality in a real project.

  Chapters 2 and 3 are hands-on, so have your computer handy.

- Part II is where the training wheels come off. Chapter 4, *Adding and Committing: Git Basics*, on page 41 deals with the basics—the commands you need to accomplish everyday tasks—getting a repository started, making commits, and so on.

  Next up, we jump into branches in Chapter 5, *Understanding and Using Branches*, on page 55. Branching is so key to how Git oper-

2. Don't worry if you don't know HTML—our project is a simple one.

ates that there's a full chapter explaining what branches are and how to use them. With the first two chapters of Part II out of the way, you'll be ready to start exploring the history of changes you've been creating. Chapter 6, *Working with Git's History*, on page 71 covers that.

Chapter 7, *Working with Remote Repositories*, on page 91 introduces you to the concepts around sharing your work with others through remote repositories. The "social" aspect of any version control system is its killer feature, and Git is no different.

Once you know how to use Git and interact with other developers' repositories, you'll learn about some organizational techniques in Chapter 8, *Organizing Your Repository*, on page 101 to keep your repository sane.

Finally, we round out Part II with Chapter 9, *Beyond the Basics*, on page 115, which introduces you to some commands you'll find useful for specialized situations.

These chapters all have lots of examples to follow along with, but keep in mind they are jumping-off points for how to use Git to work with your code's history. Once you get more comfortable, feel free to experiment.

- Part III is all about administration and is not required reading if someone else on your team or in your company handles that for you. Chapter 10, *Migrating to Git*, on page 131 shows you how to handle migration to Git from other popular VCSs, and Chapter 11, *Running a Git Server with Gitosis*, on page 143 teaches you how to administer your public repositories with Gitosis.

- We close out with a few appendixes. In Appendix A, on page 155, you'll find a command reference so you can quickly find out how to do common commands.

  In Appendix B, on page 165, you'll find coverage of some extra tools—some that ship with Git and some of which you have to install yourself—and links to online resources.

  Finally, in Appendix C, on page 173, you'll find information on other books that are referenced throughout this one.

Typographic Conventions

A few typographical conventions are used throughout this book. They are as follows:

Git	Refers to the program as a whole when capitalized.
git	Refers to the command you run on the command line.
italic	Signifies new concepts.
files and directories	Are displayed in this font.
prompt>	Comes before something you should type. Longer commands may be broken up into several lines with a \ at the end of each line. They can be typed as one line. They're broken up in the book only so they fit on the page.

Online Resources

Each chapter in Part II starts with a repository that looks like your repository does if you follow along with each of the examples throughout the book. If you skip ahead, you can get a copy of the repository by cloning it from GitHub. You can find the repositories on GitHub from my profile:

http://github.com/tswicegood

The command you need to get the current repository is listed at the start of each chapter.

The book's web page on pragprog.com[3] is a great jumping-off point for what's going on with the book. From there you can drop me a note on the forums or make suggestions or corrections on the errata page.

At this point, I'm sure you're teeming with questions. So, without further ado, let's jump into it!

3. http://www.pragprog.com/titles/tsgit

Part I

Welcome to the Distributed World

Chapter 1

Version Control the Git Way

A *version control system* (VCS) is a methodology or tool that helps you keep track of changes you make to the files in your project. In its simplest, manual form, a VCS is you creating a copy of the file you're working with and adding the date and time to the end of it.

Being pragmatic, we want something that will help automate that process. This is where VCS tools come in. They track all the changes for us, keeping a copy of every change made to the code in our projects.

Distributed version control systems (DVCSs) are no different in that respect. Their main goal is still to help us track changes we make to the projects we're working on. The difference between VCSs and DVCSs is how developers communicate their changes to each other.

In this chapter, we'll explore what a VCS is and how a DVCS—Git in particular—is different from the traditional, centralized model. You'll learn the following:

- What a repository is
- How to determine what to store
- What working trees are
- How files are manipulated and how to stay in sync
- How to track projects, directories, and their files
- How to mark milestones with tags
- How to track an alternate history with a branch
- What merging is
- How Git handles locking

All of these ideas revolve around the repository, so let's start there.

1.1 The Repository

The *repository* is the place where the version control system keeps track of all the changes you make. Most VCSs store the current state of the code, along with when each change was made, who made it, and a text log message that explains why they made the change.

You can think of a repository like a bank vault and its history like the ledger. Each time a deposit—what is called a *commit* in VCS lingo—is made, your VCS tool adds an entry to the ledger and stores the changes for safekeeping.

Originally, these repositories were accessible only if you were logged directly into the machines they were stored on. That doesn't scale, so tools such as CVS, and later Subversion, were created. They allowed developers to work remotely from the repository and send their changes back using a network connection.

These systems follow a *centralized repository* model. That means there is one central repository that everyone sends their changes to. Each developer keeps a copy of the latest version of the repository, and whenever they make a change to it, they send that change back to the main repository.

The centralized repository is an improvement over having to directly access the machine where the repository lives, but it still has limitations. First, you have only the latest version of the code. To look at the history of changes, you have to ask the repository for that information.

That brings up the second problem. You have to be able to access the remote repository—normally over a network.

In this age of always-on, broadband Internet connections, we forget that sometimes we don't have access to a network. As I've worked on this book, I've written parts at my home office, in coffee shops, on cross-country plane flights, and on the road (as a passenger) while traveling across country. I even did some of the final editing at a rustic cabin in Lake of the Ozarks, Missouri.

That highlights one of the biggest advantages of a DVCS, which is the model that Git follows. Instead of having one central repository that you and everyone else on your team sends changes to, you each have your own repository that has the entire history of the project. Making a commit doesn't involve connecting to a remote repository; the change is recorded in your local repository.

Let's go back to our bank vault analogy for a minute. A centralized system is like having one bank that every developer on your team uses. A distributed system is like each developer having their own personal bank.

You might be wondering how you can keep in sync with everyone else's changes and make sure they have yours. Each developer still sends their changes back to the main project repository. They can have access to send the changes directly to the main repository (an action called *pushing* in Git), or they might have to submit patches, which are small sets of changes, to the project's maintainer and have them update the main repository.

1.2 What Should You Store?

The short answer: everything.

The slightly less short answer: everything that you need to work on your project. Your repository needs a copy of everything in your project that's essential for you to modify, enhance, and build new versions of it.

The first and most obvious thing you should store in the repository is your project's source code. Without that, you can't fix bugs or implement new features.

Most projects have some sort of build files. A couple of common ones are Makefiles, Rakefiles, or Ant's `build.xml`. These need to be stored so you can compile your source code into something usable.

Other common items to store in your repository are sample configuration files, documentation, images that are used in the application, and of course unit tests.

Determining what to include is easy. Ask yourself, "If I didn't have X, could I do my work on this project?" If the answer is no, you couldn't, then it should be included.

Like all good rules, there is an exception. The rule doesn't apply to tools that you should use. You should include the Ant `build.xml` file but not the entire Ant program.

It's not a hard exception, though. Sometimes storing a copy of Ant or JUnit or some other program in your repository can make sure the entire team is using the same version of the tools you use. These should be stored separately from your project, however.

1.3 Working Trees

So far we've discussed the repository and talked about all the files you're storing in it, but we haven't talked about where you make all of your changes. This happens in your *working tree*.

The working tree is your current view into the repository. It has all the files from your project: the source code, build files, unit tests, and so on.

Some VCSs refer to this as your *working copy*. People coming to Git for the first time from another VCS often have trouble separating the working tree from the repository. In a VCS such as Subversion, your repository exists "over there" on another server.

In Git, "over there" means in the .git/ directory inside your project's directory on your local computer. This means you can look at the history of the repository and see what has changed without having to communicate with a repository on another server.

So, how do you get this working tree in the first place? Well, you can start your own project and then tell Git to initialize a repository for it; or you can clone an existing repository.

Cloning makes a copy of another repository and then *checks out* a copy of its master branch—its main line of development. Checking out is the process Git uses to change your working tree to match a certain point in the repository. We'll talk more about cloning repositories in Section 7.2, *Cloning a Remote Repository*, on page 94.

Of course, a VCS is all about tracking changes. So far, we've talked about repositories and your working tree—your current view of the repository—but we haven't talked about those changes yet. Now we'll cover that.

1.4 Manipulating Files and Staying in Sync

Tracking changes to your files over time is the whole reason for using a VCS. You make changes to the source code, rerun your unit tests to make sure your changes don't have any side effects, and then *commit* those changes.

Committing a change adds a new *revision* to the repository and stores your *log message* explaining what the change did. This gives you a record to go back through if you ever need to figure out why a certain change was made or when a bug was introduced.

A DVCS such as Git requires that you share your changes with other developers in order for them to have access to them. This is done by pushing the changes to an *upstream repository*.

An upstream repository is a public repository that you and possibly other developers all push changes to. Pushing is what you do when you want to send your data to another repository so it can be shared with other developers.

Pushing changes is just half of what you need to do to stay in sync. You also have to fetch changes to get the latest updates from other members on your team.

There are two steps to retrieving changes from a remote Git repository. First, you fetch them. That creates a copy of the remote repository's changes for you. This step is sort of like the reverse of pushing. Instead of sending changes to another repository, you ask the remote repository to send you the changes it has.

Next, you *merge* those changes into your local history. Git provides tools that help you merge changes. Since you normally want to fetch and merge changes at the same time, Git provides a way to do both in one step through a process called *pulling*. Pulling is similar to an update command in Subversion or CVS.

Git is fully distributed, though. You can push and pull changes to and from multiple repositories. Working with remote repositories is a core part of fully understanding how Git works. We'll cover it fully in Chapter 7, *Working with Remote Repositories*, on page 91.

1.5 Tracking Projects, Directories, and Files

So far you've seen how to store your code in repositories. In this section, we'll talk about how to organize the things you store.

At the lowest level, Git tracks the files you store in your repository as content. This is different from many version control systems that track files. Instead of tracking a models.py file, Git tracks the content—the individual characters and lines that make up the variables, functions, and so on—of models.py, and Git adds metadata to it such as the name, file mode, and whether the file is a symlink. It's a nuanced difference, but it's an important one.

Technically, this has a lot of advantages. It reduces the amount of storage space needed to store the entire history of your repository and makes it feasible and fast to do things, such as detecting functions or classes moving between two files or determining where copied code came from. We'll cover this in more detail in Section 6.5, *Following Content*, on page 79.

You interact with the data in those files exactly like you do any other files. All your work happens in the working tree. It's a set of normal directories and files that represents your current view of the repository.

The way you organize the files and directories in your repository makes up your project. Most projects follow a specific structure so everyone on the team knows where to put files so everyone else can find them.

Most companies, however, have more than one project. Some larger projects might even be broken down into several modules to make them more manageable. How you structure these modules within repositories is up to you.

Git allows you to structure your repositories however you like. You can create a new directory in the repository for each project so the projects share a common history, or you can create a new repository for each project.

Coming up with the perfect balance is challenging for someone new to the VCS world. In Chapter 8, *Organizing Your Repository*, on page 101, we'll cover some of the ways you can structure your repository.

We've covered the basics now. You know what a repository and your working tree are. You know that your project is just how you lay out the contents of your repository. Now let's explore *tags*.

1.6 Tracking Milestones with Tags

As projects progress, they hit milestones. Maybe you follow an agile methodology and have weekly development cycles where some new feature is added every week, or maybe you're on a traditional cycle where updates are released every few months.

Either way, you need to keep track of what state your repository was in when you passed that milestone. Tags give us the tool to do that. They mark a certain point in the history of the repository so you can easily reference them later.

A tag is simply a name that you can use to mark some specific point in the repository's history. It can be a major milestone such as a public release or something much more routine like the point at which a bug was fixed in your repository.

Tags help you keep track of the history of your repository by assigning an easy-to-remember name to a certain revision. Up next, we'll cover *branches*—the part of any VCS that gives you the ability to work in alternate existences.

1.7 Creating Alternate Histories with Branches

When I was a kid, one of my favorite book series was the Choose Your Own Adventure series.[1] Readers of these books will remember the way they work. You read a few pages and then make a choice. Does Joe enter the dark cave? If so, turn to page 42. Or does Joe turn around and leave the forest? If so, turn to page 23.

You can think of your repository like a book. You can read it from start to finish to get the entire story of your project. Branches are like the Choose Your Own Adventure books. There are multiple ways the story could go, each with a different history.

So, how do these alternate histories fit into your work with a version control system? Let's say you have a few ideas to rewrite a calendar component in your project. I've never worked on a project that got the calendar portion of the code right the first time, but even if it's not the calendar, there's always something on a project that can be done better with the benefit of hindsight.

To make these changes, you need to get the rest of the team on board, and then you have to track your changes. You can copy all the code into another directory and start making changes, but then there's no way to track the changes you make and—more importantly—undo the bad changes you make while experimenting.

This is where branches come in. You can create a branch that marks a point where the files in the repository diverged. Each branch keeps track of the changes made to its content separately from other branches so you can create alternate histories.

1. http://en.wikipedia.org/wiki/Choose_Your_Own_Adventure

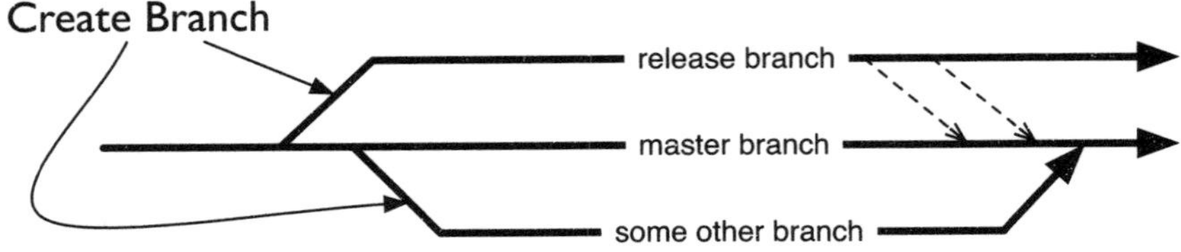

Figure 1.1: HOW BRANCHES WORK

You can see how branches work in Figure 1.1. Your master branch is the main line of development. Some other VCSs call this their *trunk*. Your branches then "branch" off that line.

The branch can exist for the rest of the project or for just a few hours. It can be merged into another branch, but there's no hard rule saying a branch has to be merged.

Sometimes, you don't even want them to merge. It might be a branch to track an older major version of your project, or it could be an experimental branch that may end up getting deleted.

Just like everything in Git, branches can be created locally without having to share them. Creating local branches and not sharing them does have its benefits. You can experiment with changes and then share them when they're something worth sharing or quietly delete them if the experiment didn't work out.

Branches and tags are an important part of working with Git. There's an entire chapter—Chapter 5, *Understanding and Using Branches*, on page 55—that covers how to use both.

Most branches need to be merged with other branches to keep them up-to-date. Up next, we'll talk about how Git handles *merging* the branches together.

1.8 Merging

In our Choose Your Own Adventure story, Joe's path when we met him had two distinct routes: into the cave or out of the forest. Often, the plot lines would come back together later in the book, though.

He might start off going through the cave but end up on the banks of the same river that flowed alongside the forest that he left. Sometimes the author runs out of places to send our hero Joe, so he has to go down the same path but get there multiple ways.

Likewise, having a couple—or even dozens—of branches is OK, but their paths will sometimes need to come together. This is where merging comes in.

Merging is taking two or more branches and combining their history into one. Git goes about merging the same way you might. It compares two sets of changes and tries to determine where changes occurred.

When changes happen in different parts of a file, Git can merge them automatically. Sometimes it can't work out what was supposed to happen, so it errs on the side of caution and tells you there's a conflict.

Say you and another developer on your team modify the same line of code but in different ways. Git sees this and can't programmatically determine which one is correct, so it flags them as a conflict and waits for you to tell it which change is correct.

Fortunately, Git has several methods of handling conflicts. Knowing how these work is an important part of mastering Git. We'll cover all of the tools you can use in Section 5.4, *Handling Conflicts*, on page 64.

With all these branches floating around and all of this talk of merging, you might be thinking "How can I keep track of what I've merged and where?"

Thankfully, you don't have to keep track. Git handles it through *merge tracking*. Just like it sounds, merge tracking keeps track of what commits have been merged together and doesn't merge them again.

This is a feature not found in many traditional VCSs such as CVS and, until recently, Subversion.[2] Without some sort of merge tracking, you have to manually keep track of what commits have been merged and where. Manually tracking merges adds to the overhead of branches and is one reason many developers have tried to avoid it in the past.

---

2. Subversion 1.5.0, which was released in June 2008, now has merge tracking.

1.9 Locking Options

When you go to the library to check out a book (not this one, because you bought a copy, right?), no one else can check it out again until you turn it back in.

The reason for this is simple: when the library has only one copy of the book, it can't physically give it to more than one person at a time. When a lot of people first hear the word *check out* and that it relates to version control, they automatically think that version control must be like a library—only one person making changes at a time.

Some VCSs do work like this. You ask the repository if you can have the settings.py file to make some changes. It says yes and then prevents everyone else from making changes until you check it back in.

This is locking at work; in particular, it's *strict locking*. Just like a library, only one person can have a copy of the code at a time. This isn't an efficient way for a team to work together, though, and doesn't fit with our DVCS model where everyone is only loosely connected to everyone else.

The alternative that most VCSs and all DVCSs use is called *optimistic locking*.[3] Optimistic locking allows multiple developers to work on the same code in the same files with the assumption that most of the time their changes won't conflict.

It works like this: Joe and Alice both create clones of the repository they share and start making changes. They both make changes to the same file but in different areas of it. Alice pushes her change back to their shared repository; then Joe attempts to push his.

Joe's attempt will be rejected, because Git detects that there has been a change on the server after he got his copy. Joe has to pull those changes from the repository, handle conflicts if there are any, and then push his change back to the server.

This all sounds incredibly complex, but it's pretty simple. You rarely have two people on the same team editing the same file, so this problem doesn't occur often. When it does, Git can handle most merges automatically.

---

3. This is sometimes referred to as *optimistic concurrency control* in the computer science world.

Configuration Management (CM)

You might have heard of tools loosely called *configuration management* (CM). They are a class of tools designed to handle the configuration of an application across multiple versions.

Many are built on top of a VCS and do support tracking the history of the configuration, but they are not version control systems by themselves.

1.10 Next Steps

We've taken a 30,000-foot view of the DVCS world and the way Git interacts with it. We've covered what repositories are, determined what we should store (nearly everything!), and talked about what working trees are. You learned how files are tracked and how repositories stay in sync, and you got an introduction to tags, branches, and the art of merging.

That gives you a basic understanding of how Git works and what a DVCS is. Up next, we'll dive into installing and configuring Git.

Chapter 2

Setting Up Git

Before you can use Git, you have to install it and do some minimal configuration. Installation is a relatively straightforward process. In this chapter, we'll do the following:

- Install Git
- Get it configured
- Introduce you to Git's GUIs
- Show you how to use Git's built-in help

Once we're finished, you'll be ready to start using Git to manage your projects.

2.1 Installing Git

If you feel comfortable with Makefiles and make is your constant companion when adding new software to your computer, you can skim most of this section. If you've never heard of any of these, don't worry—this section walks you through the process of installing Git for the first time.

Git has its heritage in the Linux world. It was originally meant to be downloaded as source code and compiled. Most modern distributions of Linux have a version of Git in their package repositories, and both Fink[1] and MacPorts[2] have Git packages. If you're on Windows, you have several options to get Git up and running, which you'll learn about in Section 2.1, *Installing on Windows*, on page 17.

1. http://www.finkproject.org/
2. http://www.macports.org/

Installing on Linux

Each distribution of Linux uses one of the various package managers available. Most distributions contain Git within their repositories, but since it is new, you may have to search through development or unstable packages to find it.

The only problem with these packages is that they tend to go out of date quite rapidly. You need to have Git version 1.6.0 or greater to follow along with the examples in this book.

For example, right now Ubuntu has the two packages you need to install Git: git-core and git-doc. However, they're both on version 1.4.4.

Instead of relying on the prebuilt version of Git in this case, I recommend downloading the latest release from Git's website[3] and compiling it yourself.

To do this in Ubuntu, you need to have the build-essential package installed. Git also has some dependencies that need to be met, but they don't change often, so you can use apt-get to grab all the dependencies with the following command:

```
prompt> sudo apt-get build-dep git-core git-doc
```

That installs all the dependencies for the git-core and git-doc packages—the same dependencies Git has when you're building from source.

Once the installation is completed, you can build Git. To do that, you need to uncompress the archive you downloaded from the Git website and switch into the directory where it's located. To build Git, type the following command:

```
prompt> make prefix=/usr/local all doc
```

That sets up Git to be installed for all users of your computer. If you want to install it for yourself, you can leave the prefix=/usr/local part out.

Compiling Git takes a few minutes. Once it's completed, you can install it by using this:

```
prompt> sudo make install install-doc
```

Once that's completed, you can run git --version from the command line to verify that Git has installed. You should see something like this:

```
prompt> git --version
git version 1.6.0.2
```

---

3. http://git.or.cz/

Check with your distribution's community and/or vendor if you're uncomfortable compiling software from source. They may be able to point you to a more up-to-date package.

Installing on OS X

If Mac OS X is more your style and you want to use a package manager, MacPorts keeps its copy of Git relatively current. To install Git using MacPorts, use the ports command from Terminal:

```
prompt> sudo port install git-core +svn +doc
```

This command installs both Git and git-svn, which we'll talk about in Chapter 10, *Migrating to Git*, on page 131.

There is also an installer package for Git that is maintained on Google Code.[4] This installs Git and also has instructions for adding an Open in Git icon to the Finder.

If you want to compile from source, you need to have Xcode,[5] the development toolkit from Apple, installed. The command for compiling Git is similar to that in the Linux section.

The only part that changes is the documentation. I would advise against adding doc and install-doc to the make commands because the dependencies can be a bit overwhelming.

Regardless of how you install Git, you can run git --version from the command line once you're finished installing to verify that it is installed:

```
prompt> git --version
git version 1.6.0.2
```

Installing on Windows

Windows support has never been at the forefront of Git development because of its roots in the Linux kernel community. With its growing popularity, people have started work on making Git completely cross-platform. If you're running Windows, you have a few options to get it up and running.

---

4. http://code.google.com/p/git-osx-installer/
5. This is available for free from http://developer.apple.com/tools/xcode/ or from the disks that came with your Mac.

Cygwin

The "official" way to run Git in Windows is to use Cygwin, a Linux emulator. This presents several issues to most Windows users, not the least of which is getting Cygwin installed and running. If Cygwin happens to be your thing, Git is available as a binary package under Devel > git: Fast Version Control System.

You need to be sure to have a few other packages as well. First, openssh from the Net category is a must because Git uses Secure Shell (SSH) as the default transfer protocol when it talks to remote repositories.

Next up, if you plan on using Git to talk to a Subversion repository like we'll discuss in Chapter 10, *Migrating to Git*, on page 131, you need to install the subversion-perl package from the Libs category. Also in that category, you should grab tcltk so you can take advantage of the integrated graphical interfaces for Git that we'll talk about in Section 2.3, *Using Git's GUI*, on page 22.

Finally, make sure to install your favorite text editor from the Editors category. Vim, emacs, or even Pico is fine, but you need to have an editor installed to take advantage of some of Git's commit log features. If you don't know what a commit log is, don't worry—you will once you're finished with the next chapter.

Git on MSys

There is a fork of Git that aims to bring Git to Windows using the underlying Windows architecture. It is not officially supported yet but is in the process of being merged back into the official Git repository.

A project has been started on Google Code called Git on MSys whose goal is to take that forked code and create an easy-to-install Git package for Windows. The installer can be downloaded from the project's website.[6]

After you download the installer, double-click it to start the installation process. The first screen displays information about the software you're about to install. You can see the screen in Figure 2.1, on the next page. Click Next to continue.

The next step is the license and any incompatibilities between the Windows version of Git and the *nix version. Since this project is aimed at Windows, there will always be slight differences, such as how line

6. http://code.google.com/p/msysgit/

Figure 2.1: WELCOME SCREEN FOR GIT INSTALLER

endings are handled. Don't worry about these changes. Any deviations from the standard Git are there to make it run better on Windows.

The next two steps are the location to install Git in and the name of the folder you want Git to create in your Start menu. The defaults are fine.

The next step is the additional enhancements you want Git on MSys to install. Leaving these at the default settings is fine.

The next step (as shown in Figure 2.2, on the following page) adds Git to your PATH environment variable. This is necessary for Windows to know where to find the git command on your system.

There are three choices. You should choose the second option. It allows you to invoke Git directly from the command line without adding any extra functionality.

Git on MSys starts the installation process now. Depending on how fast your system is, it may take a few seconds or a few minutes to finish installing. Once it has finished, you can verify that it installed correctly by running git --version from the Windows command prompt.

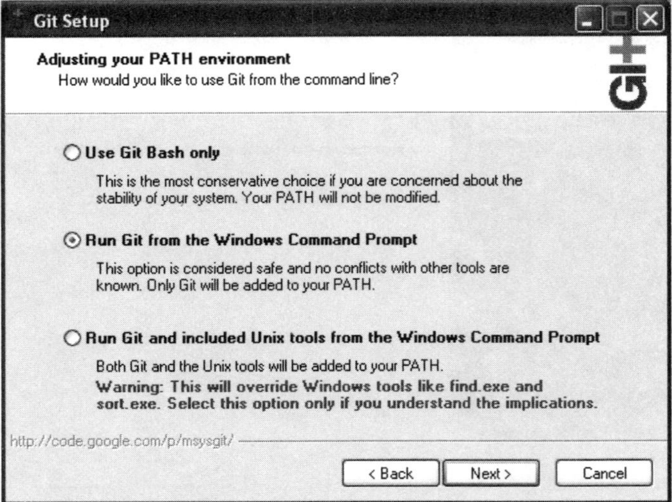

Figure 2.2: GIT EXTRAS

To start the command prompt, click Start and then Run. In the dialog box that pops up, type cmd, and click OK. Once it is started, type git --version. If everything is successful, Git outputs its version number like it does in Figure 2.3, on the next page.

Regardless of which operating system you're running, some basic configuration is necessary before you can start using Git. Let us cover that now.

2.2 Configuring Git

Git requires a few pieces of information from you to work. Since it is distributed, there's no central repository to ask what your name or email address is. You can tell Git this information by using the git config command.

To start with, we'll configure a few global values. These are the default configuration values used by every repository you create on your system. To set these configuration values as global, add the --global option.

The first two settings that must be set are user.name and user.email. The first is how you want your name to appear when you commit a change,

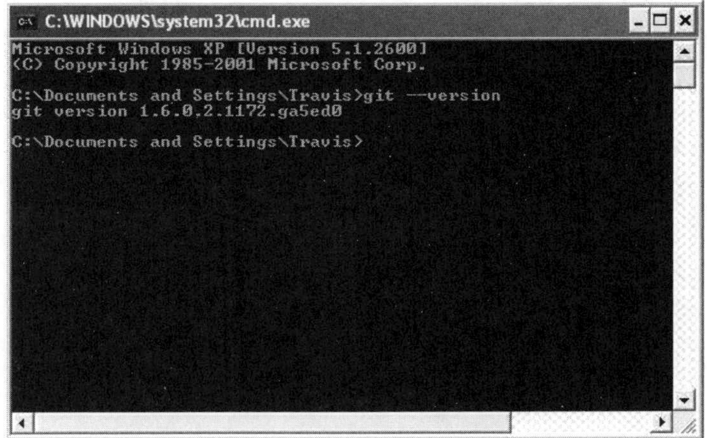

Figure 2.3: DISPLAYING THE CURRENT VERSION OF GIT IN WINDOWS

and the second is an email address that other developers can use to contact you regarding your change.

Of course, substitute your name for mine:

```
prompt> git config --global user.name "Travis Swicegood"
prompt> git config --global user.email "development@domain51.com"
```

You can verify that Git stored your settings by passing git config the --list parameter:

```
prompt> git config --global --list
user.name=Travis Swicegood
user.email=development@domain51.com
```

Those are the only two required configuration values, but Git allows you to configure more than 130 different settings.[7] Most of these you'll never need to tweak, but there is one extra change that is useful if you like color-coded output.

The setting color.ui is used to control colors in the user interface of Git. Setting it to "auto" adds color codes around the various output of Git whenever you're viewing the output in the terminal.

7. You can view a list of all the configuration settings by using the git help config command if you installed the documentation or by visiting http://www.kernel.org/pub/software/scm/git/docs/git-config.html#_variables.

You can turn this setting on with the following command:

```
prompt> git config --global color.ui "auto"
```

To me, the color-coded output is much easier to scan—especially the *diffs*, the differences between commits—but some people do prefer straight-up text, so color-coding isn't turned on by default.

That's all there is to configuring Git—you're ready to start using it. Before we jump into our project in Chapter 3, *Creating Your First Project*, on page 25, let's cover some of Git's graphical user interface (GUI) options.

2.3 Using Git's GUI

Git comes with a Tcl/Tk[8] GUI interface. You can run it from within your project's directory by typing git gui at the command prompt. Some OS-specific installers include context menu links to open git-gui—the name of the project—in the folder you are at.

git-gui provides an interface—like that in Figure 2.4, on the next page—to many of the commands we'll be discussing in this book. We won't specifically be covering the GUI interface, but if you prefer working with a GUI, you can follow along relatively closely with the examples using git-gui.

Although git-gui provides you with an interface to perform operations such as committing changes, it doesn't provide any interface for viewing the history of your repository. gitk does that. You can start it by running gitk at the command line from within your project's directory.

gitk displays the history of all the changes you make to your repository. If you want to see how the branches relate to each other, you can add the --all parameter to view all branches instead of just the current one.

One final tool that is useful if you're running Mac OS X is GitX. It's a gitk-clone, created by Pieter de Bie, that is built specifically for the Mac environment. It is hosted and available for download on its GitHub web page.[9]

We mentioned the documentation earlier when you were installing Git. Now let's cover how to access it.

---

8. Tcl/Tk is a cross-platform GUI toolkit.
9. http://gitx.frim.nl/

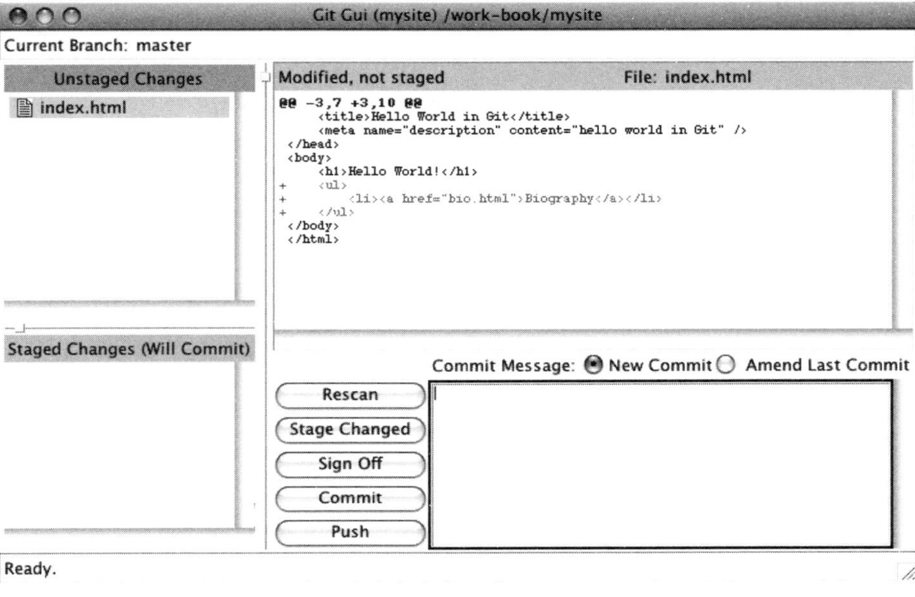

Figure 2.4: GIT-GUI RUNNING

2.4 Accessing Git's Built-in Help

Git has an extensive user manual that is available from the command line and online.[10] From the command line, you can type this:

```
prompt> git help <command>
```

Just replace <command> with the command you want help on, and Git displays the user manual entry for that command.

The documentation is not installed by default if you build from source. Some package managers distribute it as a separate git-doc package.

If you're building from source, you need to call the doc and install-doc targets when running make. Git requires AsciiDoc[11] in order to convert the documentation from plain text into the manual form.

Don't worry if you have trouble installing the documentation; you can always access it online at kernel.org, or you can download the HTML

10. http://www.kernel.org/pub/software/scm/git/docs/
11. http://www.methods.co.nz/asciidoc/

version[12] to your local computer. Look for the latest version of the git-htmldocs file.

Now you've gone through the Git installation and done the basic configuration. You have Git running, so now it's time to start using it. In the next chapter, we'll walk through a basic project so you can start to get familiar with Git.

12. http://kernel.org/pub/software/scm/git/

Chapter 3

Creating Your First Project

Now it's time to dig into Git. Up to this point, we have talked about abstract ideas and getting set up. That changes in this chapter.

We're going to work on a small HTML project and use Git to track it. Don't worry if you don't know HTML. The markup we're using here is simple and easy to follow even if you aren't familiar with HTML.

In this chapter, we'll do the following:

- Create a repository
- Add some files and make some changes
- Create a new branch
- Tag a release and clean up our repository release
- Clone a repository

Once we're finished, you'll know the basics you need to get started with Git. This chapter is a high-level overview. There are a lot of new concepts and commands introduced to get you started.

We'll be covering the commands and concepts introduced here pretty quickly, but each section has references to later parts in the book in case you can't wait to learn more about something we're talking about.

I encourage you to follow along with the examples in this chapter and the rest of the book, executing all the commands yourself. We learn via repetition, whether it's our multiplication tables in grade school or typing a Git command into the command prompt.[1]

---

1. If you're interested in the processes of learning, Andy Hunt's *Pragmatic Thinking and Learning* [Hun08] is an excellent book on the topic.

3.1 Creating a Repository

Creating a repository in Git is simple, but it seems peculiar if you're coming from Subversion or CVS. Your repository is something that exists separate from your copy of it in most VCSs. Your repository in Git is stored right alongside your working tree in a directory called .git.

To create a repository in Git, you first need to decide where you want to store your project's code. In this example, we're going to create a simple HTML page, so let's call our project *mysite*. You need to create a directory of the same name; then change into it, and type git init. The whole process should look something like this:

```
prompt> mkdir mysite
prompt> cd mysite
prompt> git init
Initialized empty Git repository in /work/mysite/.git/
```

You're done. You now have a Git repository that is ready to start tracking your project.

"But there must be more!" you cry. Actually, no. Setting up a Git repository is an extremely lightweight operation. The git init command sets up a directory called .git that stores all the repository metadata, and the empty directory we're in, mysite, serves as the working tree of code you have checked out from the repository.

3.2 Making Changes

Now that we have an empty repository, it's time to add a file to it. Create a file called index.html and add a header with the text "Hello World" in it. It should look something like this:

```
<html>
<body>
    <h1>Hello World!</h1>
</body>
</html>
```

This gives us a basic HTML page to start tracking. We'll add some more to it as we continue. Now that we have this file, it's time to tell Git we want to track it. This is a two-step process. First we have to tell Git to add the file to its index using the command git add; then we create a commit using git commit.

```
prompt> git add index.html
```

```
prompt> git commit -m "add in hello world HTML"
Created initial commit 7b1558c: add in hello world HTML
 1 files changed, 5 insertions(+), 0 deletions(-)
 create mode 100644 index.html
```

git add takes a file or the list of files you want to track as its parameter. Git has a couple of other useful ways to add files that we'll talk about in Section 4.1, *Adding Files*, on page 42.

git commit creates a *commit*. Commits are the individual pieces of history stored by the repository. Each one marks the progression of your code. Git stores your name and email address—from the configuration we did earlier—and adds a message to each commit.

That's what the -m and string in the earlier command are for. The commit message is add in hello world HTML. Properly written, log messages are the killer feature of any version control system. They're a place to explain the reason of your commit. What does the new file do? Why did you change the code? For more information writing good commit messages, check out the *Joe Asks...* on page 31.

So far, you've added a new file to the repository. You can see your commit by running git log:

```
commit 7b1558c92a7f755d8343352d5051384d98f104e4
Author: Travis Swicegood <development@domain51.com>
Date:   Sun Sep 21 14:20:21 2008 -0500

    add in hello world HTML
```

The first line here shows the commit name. Commit names are SHA-1 hashes generated by Git to keep track of a commit. Git uses these hashes to make sure that each commit identifier is completely unique, something that's important in a distributed environment. For more on why, check out the *Joe Asks...* on the following page.

You might have noticed that the commit name displayed in the git log output starts with the same seven characters as part of the output from git commit. That's because git commit shows you an abbreviated form of the commit name—the full forty-character SHA-1 hash would take up too much space.

The seven characters that are displayed by git commit are normally unique enough that you can use them without having to use the full forty-character hash. In order to keep lines short, I use the shorter form throughout the book, but git log always displays the full hash.

Joe Asks...

What Are SHA-1 Hashes, and Why Does Git Use Them?

If you're working with a centralized VCS where one server has the authority to designate one number to each commit, numbers make sense. If you're working in a distributed environment, they don't.

When two different people are working on the same code, who's to say what revision 181 is between the two of them? Git addresses this by using SHA-1 hashes.

SHA stands for Secure Hash Algorithm. It's an algorithm developed by the U.S. National Security Agency (NSA) to produce shorter strings, or *message digests*, of known data with little possibility of a "collision" with another hash.

Git generates commit names by using some metadata from the repository, your information as the person making the commit, and the current timestamp. This data combined produces a unique hash that has a small probability of ever colliding with another commit.

The possibility does exist, though, but it's low enough we can safely ignore it. For those math majors out there, or those who like trying to pronounce large numbers, the chances are 1 in 2^{63}, or 1 in 9,223,372,036,854,775,808. In American English, that's nine quintillion, two hundred twenty-three quadrillion, three hundred seventy-two trillion, thirty-six billion, eight hundred fifty-four million, seven hundred seventy-five thousand, and eight hundred and eight. And, yes, I did have to look that up.

These forty-character hashes are kind of hard to remember, though, and many times they're unnecessarily long. Most of the time the first seven or eight characters of a hash will be unique enough to match. Throughout Git, and this book, you'll see shorter commit hashes used. When Git uses smaller hashes, it uses the first seven characters.

The second line in the git log output is the commit's author info, the third is the date the commit was made, and the final bit of information is the commit log message from the commit.

3.3 Starting to Work with a Project

Now you have our repository in place, and you're already tracking your first file. Next up you have to start dealing with changes.

The HTML is missing the <head> and <title> elements. Add them. Now your index.html file should look like this:

```
<html>
<head>
    <title>Hello World in Git</title>
</head>
<body>
    <h1>Hello World!</h1>
</body>
</html>
```

You know that your file changed, and so does Git. The command git status shows you how Git sees your working tree, which is your current view of the repository. Subversion and CVS users will recognize this as their working copy.

```
prompt> git status
# On branch master
# Changed but not updated:
#   (use "git add <file>..." to update what will be committed)
#
#   modified:   index.html
#
no changes added to commit (use "git add" and/or "git commit -a")
```

This output tells us that Git sees the modification you made but doesn't know what to do with it yet. The file is listed as modified, but it's under the header Changed but not updated. To commit it, you need to *stage* the change.

Staging a commit prepares it to be committed. There are three places in Git where your code can be stored. First, the one you work with directly when editing files is the working tree.

Second is the index, which I'll refer to as the *staging area*. The staging area is a buffer between your working tree and what is stored in the repository, the third and final area in Git. You can use the staging area to stage only the changes you want to commit to the repository. We'll talk more about it in Section 4.1, *Adding Files*, on page 42.

Turn back to git add to stage the changes you just made to index.html. It is the same command you used in the previous section to add a new file. Instead of telling Git about a new file, though, it now tells Git about a new change to track.

```
prompt> git add index.html
prompt> git status
# On branch master
# Changes to be committed:
#   (use "git reset HEAD <file>..." to unstage)
#
#   modified:   index.html
#
```

In the git status command after you add the modified index.html, the header is now Changes to be committed instead of Changed but not updated. If you turned colors on, the line with index.html also changed from red to green.

Fire off a git commit command, remembering to include the -m with a commit message explaining why you made your change, and you are set:

```
prompt> git commit -m "add <head> and <title> to index" \
    -m "This allows for a more semantic document."
Created commit a5dacab: add <head> and <title> to index
 1 files changed, 3 insertions(+), 0 deletions(-)
```

Notice this time I used two -m parameters. Git accepts as many as you want to add and treats each one as a new paragraph. A quick check of git log shows the message with two paragraphs:

```
prompt> git log -1
commit a5dacabde5a622ce8ed1d1aa1ef165c46708502d
Author: Travis Swicegood <development@domain51.com>
Date:   Sun Sep 21 20:37:47 2008 -0500

    add <head> and <title> to index

    This allows for a more semantic document.
```

That also introduces a new parameter to git log, the -1. You can change the number to limit the output of git log to the number of commits you want.

We have the basics—adding new files, modifying existing ones, and looking at the repository's history—out of the way; now let's get into something meatier and turn our attention to branches.

Joe Asks...

What Should My Commit Log Message Contain?

Determining what to put in your commit log message can be tricky when you first start out. At its barest, the message should contain all the metadata explaining the "why" of the commit.

Here's a few good commit messages:

- Changed from nested if/elseif statements to switch for readability
- Removes experimental code after proven not useful

Crafting the perfect log message is something of an art. It's something that you can learn by looking at the logs of other successful projects. Git's own log is a treasure trove of excellent commit messages.

Spend a minute or two with each commit you make, and summarize the changes the same way you would as if you were explaining them to another developer sitting next to you. A great rule of thumb is to write a simple, one-line sentence that tersely explains the commit and then spend another few sentences fully explaining your commit.

Another thing to keep in mind when writing your commit message is who is going to read it. If humans are the only ones ever reading your commit messages, then straight English is fine.

If a program is going to read your log messages, you need to make sure you're including all the information it expects. There are tools that can read commit logs and update third-party tools such as ticket-tracking systems to show activity on tasks.

Adding Some Color to Git's Output

If you turned colors on in your configuration, you probably noticed the color the first time you ran git status. Unstaged modifications—modifications that Git doesn't know what to do with—appear in red. Once you stage the changes with git add, they will change to green.

3.4 Using and Understanding Branches

Branches are a way to maintain alternate histories of the project you're working on, like we talked about in Section 1.7, *Creating Alternate Histories with Branches*, on page 9. Alternate histories are great, but how do we use them in a real project?

The honest answer is "any way you want." For our purposes, though, we'll narrow it down a bit. Two types of branches are useful: different versions of a project in different branches and topic branches that deal with a specific feature. In this section, we'll talk about the first kind of branches.

Your mysite code is almost ready to be released, but it still needs to be signed off on by everyone involved. In the meantime, you can start working on the new features in the next version.

You can use a branch to keep a copy of your code that's ready to release so you don't have to stop developing. The command to create a branch is git branch, and it takes two parameters: the name of the branch you want to create and the name of the branch you want to create it from:

```
prompt> git branch RB_1.0 master
```

That command creates a branch called RB_1.0 from the master branch. master is the name of the default branch in Git. CVS and Subversion users might recognize this as the trunk in those VCSs.

The RB in the branch name stands for *release branch*. Adding the prefix makes it easier for you and other developers to quickly determine what branches are release branches.

Now you can start making changes without affecting the code that's almost ready for a release. Next up is adding a link to a bio page. Right before the closing </body> tag, add this:

```
<ul>
    <li><a href="bio.html">Biography</a></li>
</ul>
```

Commit your changes now, except this time use the following command:

```
prompt> git commit -a
... editor launch, create log message, save, and exit ...
Created commit e993d25: add in a bio link
 1 files changed, 3 insertions(+), 0 deletions(-)
```

Notice that this time the command has the -a parameter on it. That tells Git to commit all files that it knows about that have changed.

Now you have a change on your master branch that is not included on your release branch. Let's switch to the release branch and make the final change to it before it's ready for release. The command to switch is git checkout.

```
prompt> git checkout RB_1.0
Switched to branch "RB_1.0"
```

If you had your index.html file open, your editor is probably complaining about the file changing. Go ahead and reload the file. Now your changes from the master branch have been removed—they're still safely stored, in the other branch.

The final change that needs to be added to your file before it can be released is a description metatag. Add a description so the code in your <head> block looks something like this:

```
<head>
    <title>Hello World in Git</title>
    <meta name="description" content="hello world in Git" />
</head>
```

Save and commit your changes:

```
prompt> git commit -a
... editor launch, create log message, save, and exit ...
Created commit 4b53779: Add in a description element to the metadata
 1 files changed, 1 insertions(+), 0 deletions(-)
```

Now it's ready to release. Now it's time to mark the release with a tag.

3.5 Handling Releases

Your code is ready for its 1.0 release. It's time to tag it. Tagging code in Git marks a specific point in the history of the repository so you can refer to it easily. Since this is the 1.0 release, tag it with that number:

```
prompt> git tag 1.0 RB_1.0
```

The two parameters specify the name of the tag and the point you want to tag: 1.0 and the branch RB_1.0, respectively. You can view a list of tags in your repository by running git tag without any parameters. Right now, it shows only the 1.0 tag you just created:

```
prompt> git tag
1.0
```

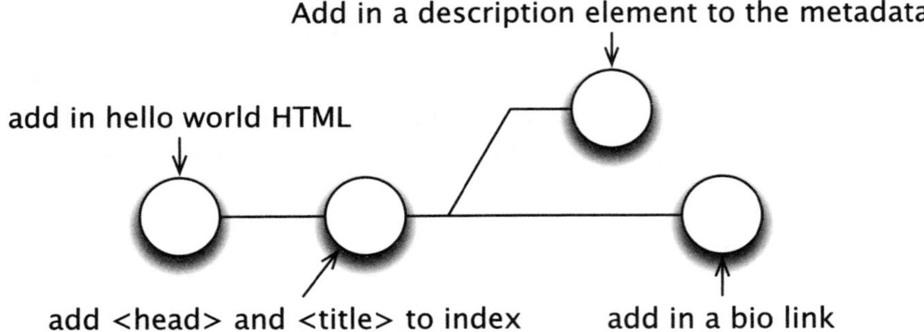

Figure 3.1: MYSITE REPOSITORY BEFORE REBASE

Now that your code is tagged, you need to perform some cleanup. You have two branches, and each contains commits that the other does not know about. The master branch—the branch you started working on 2.0 features in—needs to know about the new <meta> code you added in RB_1.0.

To do this, use the git rebase command. Rebasing takes the changes from a branch and replays them on top of another branch. Right now your repository looks like Figure 3.1. After rebasing, it looks like Figure 3.2, on the facing page.

First, you need to switch back to the master branch. That's the git checkout command from earlier.

```
prompt> git checkout master
Switched to branch "master"
```

Next, you can run the git rebase command. For our purposes right now, it takes one parameter: the name of the branch you want to rebase against.

```
prompt> git rebase RB_1.0
First, rewinding head to replay your work on top of it...
Applying: add in a bio link
```

Now your repository looks like Figure 3.2, on the next page. The add in a bio link is now placed after the final commit in the RB_1.0 branch.

Now, for the final piece of cleanup—deleting the release branch. This might seem drastic, but don't worry. The tag you just created points

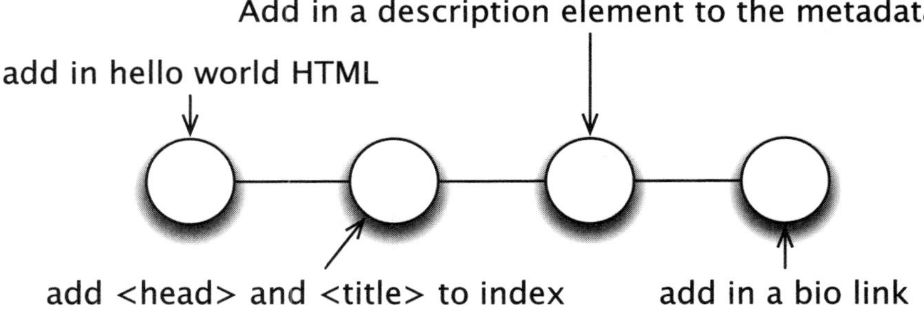

Figure 3.2: MYSITE REPOSITORY AFTER REBASE

to the same commit that the RB_1.0 branch does, so everything is still intact.

You use git branch to delete the branch by adding the -d parameter before the branch name:

```
prompt> git branch -d RB_1.0
Deleted branch RB_1.0.
```

So, how do you handle creating patches to the 1.0.*x* branch if you don't keep the release branch around? That's easy—create a branch off the tag you created.

Remember when you created the branch earlier? You gave it the name of the branch you wanted to create the branch from. Just change that to the tag, and you're set:

```
prompt> git branch RB_1.0.1 1.0
prompt> git checkout RB_1.0.1
Switched to branch "RB_1.0.1"
```

A quick check of git log shows that you have only the three commits that were in your RB_1.0 branch:

```
prompt> git log --pretty=oneline
4b53779 Add in a description element to the metadata
a5dacab add <head> and <title> to index
7b1558c add in hello world HTML
```

There's one final piece of the release puzzle that Git can help you with: creating an archive of your release. You don't always need to distribute the history of your project with your releases. Often, a tarball or zip file of it at the point you tag is enough. Git provides the git archive command to do that.

This is how you create a gzipped tarball of mysite:

```
prompt> git archive --format=tar \
                    --prefix=mysite-1.0/ 1.0 \
                    | gzip > mysite-1.0.tar.gz
```

There are three parameters here. First, --format tells Git to generate tar output. Second, --prefix tells Git to put everything in the mysite-1.0/ directory. Finally, 1.0 tells Git to use that tag to determine what to store in the archive.

The third line gets a little more complicated if you're not used to Unix-style commands. It pipes the output from git archive—a tar file—to gzip, which compresses the file. The output is then sent to the mysite-1.0.tar.gz file that you can distribute.

git archive also lets you create zip files. Creating zip files is a little more straightforward because the output from git archive is already compressed. You can use the following command to create a zip file:

```
prompt> git archive --format=zip \
                    --prefix=mysite-1.0/ 1.0 \
                    > mysite-1.0.zip
```

The parameters are almost the same between the zip and tar formats. The value you pass to --format changes, and instead of piping the output through gzip, with zips you send it directly to the file where you want to save it.

Of course, there's often more to handling a release—you might have wiki pages to update, acceptance tests to run against the code, and so on—but every one of those tasks is dependent on the tools and methods you use.

By using tags, you can manage how Git interacts with those processes you have, and Git's archive command can help you create the releases of your project's source code.

That wraps up the basic commands, but so far we've covered only the commands that you use locally. Next we'll cover *cloning*, which is what you need to get a project from someone remotely.

3.6 Cloning a Remote Repository

One thing we haven't touched on yet is remote repositories. You've built up the mysite repository using commands that interact locally. Git can also deal with remote repositories, however, so you can share your work and get copies of others' repositories.

To get started with a remote repository, you need to clone it using the git clone command. Cloning a remote repository does what it sounds like. It creates a complete copy of the remote repository that you can start working with.

I already have my copy of mysite shared on GitHub, a Git repository hosting service. You can try the git clone command by creating a clone of it:

```
prompt> cd /work
prompt> git clone git://github.com/tswicegood/mysite.git mysite-remote
Initialized empty Git repository in /work/mysite-remote/.git/
remote: Counting objects: 12, done.
remote: Compressing objects: 100% (8/8), done.
remote: Total 12 (delta 2), reused 0 (delta 0)
Receiving objects: 100% (12/12), done.
Resolving deltas: 100% (2/2), done.
```

git clone takes two parameters—the location of the repository you want to clone and the directory where you want the repository to live. The second is optional, but you already have a mysite directory, so you need to provide the second parameter to put it in a directory of its own.

That's all there is to cloning. You can provide some additional parameters that we'll talk about in Section 7.2, *Cloning a Remote Repository*, on page 94, but the majority of times you create a clone, providing the location and the directory you want to store the clone in is all you need to do.

Of course, you can push and fetch changes as well. We're going to save those for later, though, once you're more comfortable working with your local repository. There's a whole chapter—Chapter 7, *Working with Remote Repositories*, on page 91—devoted to working with remote repositories.

Are you dizzy yet? In this chapter, you learned the basics of Git—git add, git commit, git status, and git log. We built on that foundation and talked about git branch, git tag, and git rebase, as well as got a quick glimpse of git clone.

Part I has been a lightning-fast tour of the concepts of VCS/DVCS and Git. This chapter particularly has been heavy on commands but thin on the "why" of the various commands. Working through the exercise in this chapter, you've used Git to manage a simple repository for your HTML page project.

Now it's time to step back, start with the basics, and build up your knowledge of what Git is doing. In the coming chapters, we'll continue to build on the mysite repository as we explore even more of Git.

Part II

Everyday Git

Chapter 4

Adding and Committing: Git Basics

Now it's time to dig into Git. Part I introduced you to Git; Part II is about specifics. We'll dig into Git and go through the basic commands you need in your day-to-day use of Git.

This chapter focuses on a few areas that we touched on in Chapter 3, *Creating Your First Project*, on page 25. You'll now get a much deeper understanding of the following:

- Adding files
- Creating commits
- Checking on what has changed
- Managing files

We'll be building on the repository we started in Chapter 3, *Creating Your First Project*, on page 25. If you skipped ahead to this point, don't worry—you can always clone the repository to get the repository that I built:

```
prompt> git clone git://github.com/tswicegood/mysite.git
Initialized empty Git repository in /work/mysite/.git/
remote: Counting objects: 12, done.
remote: Compressing objects: 100% (8/8), done.
remote: Total 12 (delta 2), reused 0 (delta 0)
Receiving objects: 100% (12/12), done.
Resolving deltas: 100% (2/2), done.
```

Now that you have your repository—either the one you created in the previous chapter or by cloning mine—you're ready to start.

4.1 Adding Files

You're constantly adding new files and making changes to your repository's contents. git add fills both of these roles. Just give it the name of a file or the files you want to add, and Git stages the changes to commit.

Before we proceed, there is a little terminology to clear up. *Staged changes* are simply changes in your working tree that you want to tell your repository about. When you stage a change, it updates what Git refers to as its *index*. A lot of people, myself included, refer to it as the *staging area*.

The staging area is just that, a place where you can set up commits prior to committing to your repository.

"But isn't this double the amount of work? Why can't I just commit?"

In a lot of cases, yes, it is double work and there are shortcuts that we'll talk about in the next section to get around it, but don't forget about the staging area. It gives you the ability to craft exactly the commit you want to make prior to making it. To be able to craft the changes, though, you have to add them first. git add is the command for that.

Like all good Git commands, there's more to adding files than just calling git add. You can specify several different options to change how git add behaves, and a couple of the options are even useful.

You can use Git's interactive add mode to select which files or parts of files to stage for a commit. You start it by adding the -i option.

This starts up the interactive shell for staging changes, adding new files, and even staging part of a file. Let's change the index.html file so we have something to stage. Change the Biography link to About. It now looks like this:

```
<li><a href="about.html">About</a></li>
```

Now, run git add -i. Git displays a prompt like the following one when you start up interactive mode:

```
prompt> git add -i
           staged     unstaged path
  1:    unchanged        +1/-1 index.html

*** Commands ***
  1: status   2: update       3: revert       4: add untracked
  5: patch    6: diff         7: quit         8: help
What now>
```

You have several options now. Typing 1 generates this same status that is shown when you start up. To add a file, you can type 2 to stage the file:

```
What now> 2
           staged     unstaged path
  1:    unchanged        +1/-1 index.html
Update>>
```

This generates a list of files that can be staged. In this case, there's one file to add, so type 1, and it will change to having an asterisk (*) beside its name to signify that it's going to be staged:

```
Update>> 1
           staged     unstaged path
* 1:    unchanged        +1/-1 index.html
Update>>
```

Once you're ready to leave this mode, you can press Enter to return to the main menu:

```
Update>>
updated one path

*** Commands ***
  1: status   2: update      3: revert      4: add untracked
  5: patch    6: diff        7: quit        8: help
What now>
```

Now checking the status again, you can see that there's one change staged and nothing listed in the unstaged changes:

```
What now> 1
           staged     unstaged path
  1:        +1/-1      nothing index.html

*** Commands ***
  1: status   2: update      3: revert      4: add untracked
  5: patch    6: diff        7: quit        8: help
What now>
```

You can use the revert functionality if you need to unstage a change. It works just like the update we did a few paragraphs ago:

```
What now> 3
           staged     unstaged path
  1:        +1/-1      nothing index.html
Revert>> 1
           staged     unstaged path
* 1:        +1/-1      nothing index.html
Revert>>
reverted one path
```

```
*** Commands ***
  1: status   2: update       3: revert       4: add untracked
  5: patch    6: diff         7: quit         8: help
What now>
```

Running status will show that the changes have gone to unstaged now:

```
What now> 1
           staged     unstaged path
  1:    unchanged        +1/-1 index.html

*** Commands ***
  1: status   2: update       3: revert       4: add untracked
  5: patch    6: diff         7: quit         8: help
```

If you want to stage files that are not being tracked yet, you can use the fourth option. It works like the others, so I won't show it again.

Patch mode is the most useful feature of interactive mode. It starts out like the other modes. You can choose which file or files you want to add via patch mode. Once you make your choice, you are presented with a diff of the changed files and given the option to add the changes or not. It looks something like this:

```
What now> 5
           staged     unstaged path
  1:    unchanged        +1/-1 index.html
Patch update>> 1
           staged     unstaged path
* 1:    unchanged        +1/-1 index.html
Patch update>>
diff --git a/index.html b/index.html
index e812d0a..ca86894 100644
--- a/index.html
+++ b/index.html
@@ -6,7 +6,7 @@
 <body>
     <h1>Hello World!</h1>
     <ul>
-        <li><a href="bio.html">Biography</a></li>
+        <li><a href="about.html">About</a></li>
     </ul>
 </body>
 </html>
Stage this hunk [y/n/a/d/e/?]?
```

Now you have the option of adding this *hunk* or denying it. A hunk is a change within the file. Consecutive changes are treated as one hunk. Each different area in a file is treated as its own hunk.

From the prompt, typing y accepts the change, n skips it, and a and d add or deny all the rest of the changes in the file. Don't worry about trying to remember all these commands right now. There's a ? that displays some help explaining what all the options do when you're looking at a hunk.

For now, type n to skip staging that hunk, and then press 7 to exit interactive mode:

```
Stage this hunk [y/n/a/d/e/?]? n

*** Commands ***
  1: status   2: update       3: revert       4: add untracked
  5: patch    6: diff         7: quit         8: help
What now> 7
Bye.
```

Like all the most useful features in Git, there's a shortcut to going straight to patch mode without launching interactive mode. You can add -p to git add to start directly in patch mode.

For example, you can run the following to launch patch mode directly on index.html:

```
prompt> git add -p
diff --git a/index.html b/index.html
index e812d0a..ca86894 100644
--- a/index.html
+++ b/index.html
@@ -6,7 +6,7 @@
 <body>
     <h1>Hello World!</h1>
     <ul>
-        <li><a href="bio.html">Biography</a></li>
+        <li><a href="about.html">About</a></li>
     </ul>
 </body>
 </html>
Stage this hunk [y/n/a/d/e/?]?
```

This time, enter y to select the hunk. Now it's staged and ready to commit, which brings us to committing changes.

4.2 Committing Changes

Committing is a relatively straightforward process that adds your changes to the history of your repository and assigns a commit name to them.

Tracking Empty Directories

Git doesn't track directories. There has been some historical resistance to the idea of tracking empty directories. The theory goes that most well-maintained projects don't actually need empty directories.

That may change in the future and Git might track directories, but in the meantime, there is an easy workaround if you need to store an empty directory. Just add an empty file in the directory you want to track, and add it to your repository.

You can name the file anything you want, but most people start the file's name with a period (.) because most file systems ignore files that begin with a period.

The change is not sent to a central repository, though. Other people can pull the change from you, or you can push the change to some other repository, but there's no automatic updating. We'll talk about these in Section 7.3, *Keeping Up-to-Date*, on page 95 and Section 7.4, *Pushing Changes*, on page 96.

You can use git commit in multiple ways to commit changes to your repository, but every commit requires a log message. For simple messages, you can add a message by adding -m "your message". The message can be any valid string. You can also specify multiple paragraphs by passing multiple -m options to git commit.

For more complex messages that require an editor, you can execute git commit without the -m, and Git launches your editor to create your log message. When Git tries to launch an editor, it looks through the following values in this order:

1. GIT_EDITOR environment variable.
2. core.editor Git configuration value.
3. VISUAL environment variable.
4. EDITOR environment variable.
5. Git tries vi if nothing else is set.

When you use the editor to create your commit message, by adding the -v option you can tell Git to add a diff in the editor showing the changes you are about to commit. There will be a lot of lines that begin with #. All of those are ignored when Git reads the commit message.

Like nearly every command in Git, there are a few different ways to handle a commit. Before we create a new commit, let's look at the three ways to generate a commit.

First, you can call git add in some form for the files—or changes if you're using git add -p—that you want to commit. This stages those changes for commit, and calling git commit closes the loop. The process looks like this:

```
prompt> git add some-file
prompt> git commit -m "changes to some-file"
```

That's an example of a bad commit log message, but it does fit nicely on a printed page, so I'll use it here as an example. In a real commit message, don't just state the obvious—make sure to explain why you made the changes too. Remember from the *Joe Asks...* on page 31 that your commit message should explain the commit like you would to a developer sitting right next to you.

Another way to handle commits is to pass git commit the -a parameter on the command line. It tells Git to take the most current version of your working tree and commit it to the repository. It won't add new, untracked files, however—only files that are already being tracked.

If the only change you had made to your working tree in the previous example was to some-file, you could perform the same commit by executing the following:

```
prompt> git commit -m "changes to some-file" -a
```

The last method of committing changes is to specify the file or files you want to commit. Just add each file you want to commit after you specify all the options you want to pass Git.

Like the -a parameter, this takes the latest version from your working tree. But it takes just the file or files you specify. Here's an example from the two previous commits:

```
prompt> git commit -m "changes to some-file" some-file
```

All three examples have their uses. Staged commits are useful when you want to commit a portion of a file using the git add -p command. If you need to pull one file out of several that have changed and commit that, you can commit using the explicit file.

Using Git Aliases Like SVN Shortcuts

If you're coming from Subversion, you are probably used to all those shortcuts to commonly used commands. You never have to type svn checkout or svn commit because a simple svn co or svn ci does the trick for you.

Reading through this book and trying the examples, you might have tried those same aliases with Git and got an error that you weren't using a Git command. Git doesn't ship with all those aliases like Subversion, but it does give you a better option. You can add your own aliases via git config.

You can add git ci as a shortcut to git commit with the following:

```
prompt> git config --global alias.ci "commit"
```

That works for any Git command, so you can customize your environment just the way you want it. Substitute the portion after alias. for the alias you want to create, and you're set.

There is an important difference to remember between the first method of committing staged commits and committing all changes or a particular file's changes. The last two methods commit the file as it exists the moment you execute the commit. The first method commits the change you staged.

This means you can stage a change, make a change to the file, and then commit the change you staged while still having a file that is changed in your working tree.

Think of a staged area as a buffer. You add to the buffer with git add. That buffer stays there until you save it by executing git commit.

Speaking of staged commits, you still have that change staged from the previous section. Let's leave it there for a little bit longer while we explore various ways to view what has changed in your repository.

4.3 Seeing What Has Changed

It's easy to remember that you added a new file or made a change to one file when it's fresh in your mind. Sometimes you don't have that luxury, though. Someone walks into your office or you get caught up in preparation for an impending deadline right after you stage a change.

You need to find out what has changed in your working tree and how it has changed. You can use two of Git's commands, git status and git diff, to do that.

Viewing the Current Status

You can use git status to see all the changes that have occurred in your repository. The output it generates is based on the status of any staged commits and how your current working copy compares to what is tracked by the repository.

There's still that change you staged earlier. You can see it right now with git status:

```
prompt> git status
# On branch master
# Changes to be committed:
#   (use "git reset HEAD <file>..." to unstage)
#
#       modified:   index.html
#
```

Note that it has the header Changes to be committed. That tells you that it's waiting to be committed. Let's add another change. This time add a Contact link after the About link. Here's the new line I added:

```
<li><a href="contact.html">Contact</a></li>
```

After you've saved your change, run git status again:

```
prompt> git status
# On branch master
# Changes to be committed:
#   (use "git reset HEAD <file>..." to unstage)
#
#       modified:   index.html
#
# Changed but not updated:
#   (use "git add <file>..." to update what will be committed)
#
#       modified:   index.html
#
```

Now there's two index.html files listed. The first one is the change you staged earlier. You can tell this because of that header—Changes to be committed. The second one is the change you just made. It hasn't been staged yet, so it has the Changed but not updated header above it. The first will be green and the second red if you turned on color.ui back in Section 2.2, *Configuring Git*, on page 20.

You just made the changes, so I'm sure you still remember what they are. Sometimes you need to see, though. To do that, you can check the diffs—the differences—between the files.

Viewing Difference

Git can show you the differences between what's in your working tree, what's staged and ready to be committed, and what's in your repository. You use the git diff command to do this.

Calling git diff with no parameters shows you the changes in your working tree that you haven't staged or committed yet.

```
prompt> git diff
diff --git a/index.html b/index.html
index ca86894..5fdc539 100644
--- a/index.html
+++ b/index.html
@@ -7,6 +7,7 @@
     <h1>Hello World!</h1>
     <ul>
         <li><a href="about.html">About</a></li>
+        <li><a href="contact.html">Contact</a></li>
     </ul>
 </body>
 </html>
```

That shows you the Contact link you added—the + at the beginning of the line shows that it's an addition—but something is missing. The About link doesn't show any change.

Running git diff without any parameters compares the changes in your working tree against the staging area. You know that there are changes there, though. git status shows that something is staged. View the differences in the staging area and the repository by adding --cached to the call:

```
prompt> git diff --cached
diff --git a/index.html b/index.html
index e812d0a..ca86894 100644
--- a/index.html
+++ b/index.html
@@ -6,7 +6,7 @@
 <body>
     <h1>Hello World!</h1>
     <ul>
-        <li><a href="bio.html">Biography</a></li>
+        <li><a href="about.html">About</a></li>
     </ul>
 </body>
 </html>
```

Now you see that change you made back in Section 4.1, *Adding Files*, on page 42. Notice that there's a - in front of the Biography line. This shows you that the line is being removed. If colors are on, Git also marks the deleted content as red, and added content is green.

That diff doesn't show the changes that aren't staged yet, though. You can compare everything that's in your working tree—including your staged changes—against what's in your repository. To do that, execute git diff, and add HEAD to the end:

```
prompt> git diff HEAD
diff --git a/index.html b/index.html
index e812d0a..5fdc539 100644
--- a/index.html
+++ b/index.html
@@ -6,7 +6,8 @@
 <body>
     <h1>Hello World!</h1>
     <ul>
-        <li><a href="bio.html">Biography</a></li>
+        <li><a href="about.html">About</a></li>
+        <li><a href="contact.html">Contact</a></li>
     </ul>
 </body>
 </html>
```

HEAD is a keyword that refers to the most recent commit to the branch you're in. You don't need to worry about that branch part just yet, but it does come back up.

Let's create a commit so our changes are tracked:

```
prompt> git commit -a -m "Change biography link and add contact link" \
    -m "About is shorter, so easier to process" \
    -m "We need to provide contact info"
Created commit 6f1bf6f: Change biography link and add contact link
 1 files changed, 2 insertions(+), 1 deletions(-)
```

Now you know all the normal commands to get you going. You can add files, commit changes to the files you're tracking, and even compare the changes you've made against what's in your repository. Let's get into some housecleaning commands now such as moving, copying, and even ignoring some files.

4.4 Managing Files

Now your repository is starting to come together. With one file, it's pretty simple right now, but as it grows, some cleanup is necessary.

Files need moving, code needs to be copied around, and some of the everyday cruft from working with your project needs to be ignored.

Renaming and Moving Files

We all write flawless, bug-free code on our first pass. Right? Even though we would like to think that we do, we sometimes get things wrong. Naming a file incorrectly or putting it in the wrong directory is no exception.

You can move a file in Git by typing git mv <original-file> <new-file>. The command tells Git to create new-file with the existing file's content, and it keeps the history and removes original-filename.

Your "Hello World" page is not an index, so let's move it:

```
prompt> git mv index.html hello.html
prompt> git status
# On branch master
# Your branch is ahead of 'origin/master' by 1 commit.
#
# Changes to be committed:
#   (use "git reset HEAD <file>..." to unstage)
#
#   renamed:    index.html -> hello.html
#
```

git mv is a convenience. Git can detect the movement of a file, but more steps are involved. You have to move the file and then call git add on the new file and git rm—the command to remove a file from the repository—on the old file.

Go ahead and commit the new hello.html move:

```
prompt> git commit -m "rename to more appropriate name"
Created commit 9a23464: rename to more appropriate name
 1 files changed, 0 insertions(+), 0 deletions(-)
 rename index.html => hello.html (100%)
```

Now that you've renamed the index.html file, let's talk about copying files.

Copying Files—or Not

If you're used to Subversion, you might find it odd that Git doesn't have a git cp command for copying. There's a reason—Git doesn't need it.

Subversion's copy is mainly to let you create branches and tags—Git provides you with the commands to handle both of those directly. Git does track copied code, though.

That brings us to a point we haven't talked much about yet. Git doesn't track files; it tracks content like we talked about in Section 1.5, *Tracking Projects, Directories, and Files*, on page 7.

Git has a good reason for this. Filenames are nothing more than metadata added to the content of files so they can be organized. Git can figure out that name by asking the file system about it, but what it cares about is the content that's stored inside files.

So, how does this all apply to copying files? Since Git tracks only content, it can detect when the same content is duplicated across multiple commits without you having to explicitly tell it to copy.

You can view the copied code, something we'll cover in Section 6.5, *Following Content*, on page 79. Be careful, though. If you find yourself copying a lot of code around, it might be a sign that your code needs to be refactored[1] to avoid duplication.

Ignoring Files

Depending on your editor, you might be seeing slightly different output from git status. Actually, that's because I changed my repository and didn't tell you about it.

This is what my output looks like when I remove that change and run git status:

```
prompt> git status
# On branch master
# Your branch is ahead of 'origin/master' by 2 commits.
#
# Untracked files:
#   (use "git add <file>..." to include in what will be committed)
#
#       .index.html.swp
nothing added to commit but untracked files present
(use "git add" to track)
```

My favorite editor is MacVim.[2] Whenever I start editing a file with it, it creates an .swp file for internal tracking. That's cruft that doesn't need to be in the repository. You can ignore it by adding it to the .gitignore file, and it disappears.

1. Refactoring is the "art" of making code better by small incremental changes. For a thorough introduction to the topic, there is no better source than Martin Fowler's book *Refactoring* [FBB+99].
2. http://code.google.com/p/macvim/

Adding one file at a time to ignore is inefficient, so Git allows wildcards. Since I know that MacVim swap files always begin with a period and end with .swp, I add .*.swp to the .gitignore, and Git ignores all matching files:

```
... add ".*.swp" to .gitignore file ...
prompt> git status
# On branch master
# Untracked files:
#   (use "git add <file>..." to include in what will be committed)
#
#       .gitignore
nothing added to commit but untracked files present
(use "git add" to track)
```

Now the swap file is gone and replaced with the new .gitignore. It's a regular file that can be tracked and distributed with your repository, so everyone who clones your work will ignore those files as well.

Every developer has their own favorite editor, though, and each one uses a different mechanism to save backups and signify that it has a file open. Distributing your personal preferences as part of the repository might not be such a good idea.

You can tell your local repository to ignore files like these without sharing the exclusion with everyone else. Edit the file .git/info/exclude, and add your rules there.

Deciding Where to Ignore

You can decide what to ignore at the repository level through .gitignore and what to ignore locally through .git/info/exclude by asking yourself a simple question: Is this kind of file something that everyone is going to have in their repositories?

If the answer to that is yes, you need to ignore it by adding the rule to the .gitignore file and committing that file to the repository. If it's only a file you'll see, add it to your .git/info/exclude file.

Since I didn't want to add an extra file and commit to the repository, I had the .*.swp line added to my .git/info/exclude file.

We've covered the basics now in this chapter. Everything else builds on these basics. Start *adding* things to your repository, and then *commit* your changes.

Now you have the basics down. Now it's time to start learning about branches. Other VCSs treat them as an afterthought, but in Git they're so important to use that we need to cover them up front.

Chapter 5

Understanding and Using Branches

You can use Git with a single branch—the default master—and get all the benefits of a VCS. Git will track the history, let you collaborate with other developers, and make sure you don't accidentally delete something important.

But using Git this way is like buying a racing car and using it for your commute. It will get you there, but you never get to use the car to its potential in the 8 a.m. rush-hour traffic.

Branches are a fundamental part of Git. In this chapter, you'll learn what branches are and how to do the following:

- Create new branches
- Merge changes between branches
- Handle conflicts
- Delete branches
- Rename branches
- Handle release branches

We're going to be working with the repository that you've created up to this point. If you've skipped ahead, you can clone the repository from its GitHub repository:

```
prompt> git clone git://github.com/tswicegood/mysite-chp4.git
Initialized empty Git repository in /work/mysite-chp4/.git/
```

5.1 What Are Branches?

We all have competing priorities at work that we have to juggle. Adding new features, refactoring existing code to make it more maintainable, and fixing the occasional bug—they all jockey for our attention, and we have to balance them.

A straight, linear history has a hard time coping with these demands. This is where branches come in. We talked about them in Section 1.7, *Creating Alternate Histories with Branches*, on page 9. They allow you to track changes with different histories.

Here is Git's secret: *everything* is treated like a branch. So far, all the work you've been doing has been in the master branch, but nothing is stopping you from giving it another name. Actually, let's do that:

```
prompt> git branch -m master mymaster
prompt> git branch
* mymaster
```

That's it. You renamed the master branch to mymaster. Both of the commands use git branch, but they provide different parameters.

The first has three parameters. The -m parameter tells Git to perform a move. The other two parameters are the old branch name and the new name you want your branch to have.

The second command is git branch by itself. Git displays the names of all the local branches in your repository when it isn't given any parameters. Git just shows the one branch name here since this repository has only one branch.

Just to tidy things up, let's rename it to master:

```
prompt> git branch -m mymaster master
```

Since everything is considered a branch in Git, they're "cheap." Unlike other systems where all the files are copied into a new directory, a branch in Git tracks the commits that were made to it from the point it was created.

Actually, that's a little white lie. Git's branches keep track of only the most recent commit to that branch. That commit has a link to its parent, and using that link Git can figure out all the changes in that branch.[1]

1. Those with a background in computer science or mathematics might recognize this as a directed acyclic graph (DAG).

One of the hardest parts of branches is figuring out when to create a branch. It's an art, not a science. Here are a few of things that I create new branches for:

- *Experimental changes*: Want to try rewriting algorithms just to see whether they're faster, or want to try refactoring a section of code to a particular pattern? Create a new branch to do your work in, and you can work on it separately from any changes that are being deployed immediately.
- *New features*: Every time you start working on a new feature, create a new branch. You can merge it back in as soon as you're done, either with the full history or through a squashed commit. We'll talk about these different merging strategies in Section 5.3, *Merging Changes Between Branches*, on page 59.
- *Bug fixes*: Whether it's a fix to a bug in code that hasn't been released or code that has already been tagged for a release, you can create a branch to track your changes to that bug. This gives you a lot of flexibility in how you merge it back into the rest of the code, just like creating a branch for a new feature. This is especially true if your bug fix is going to take some experimentation.

How you create and use your branches depends a lot on the project. I used Git to track all the changes to this book and employed a pretty extensive branch strategy.

My beta branch contained the latest copy of the book with the content that was ready to ship, and each chapter had its own branch. New edits to the chapters happened in their own branch, and then I merged those changes back in to the beta branch once they were ready.

I also employed a lot of temporary branches. For example, every time I fixed errata I would create an errata branch, make the corrections, merge the changes back in, and delete the branch.

That gives you the high-level view of branches and introduces you to some basics about them. Now, let's start creating new branches.

5.2 Creating a New Branch

Creating a new branch is a simple process. You still use the git branch command, except this time you give it the name of the new branch you want to create. You can create a branch called new like this:

```
prompt> git branch new
```

Git doesn't give us any visible feedback that it created a new branch, but we can check by running git branch again without any parameters:

```
prompt> git branch
* master
  new
```

There's our new branch called new. Notice that the master branch has an asterisk by its name. That's to signify which branch is currently *checked out*. The checked-out branch is the branch that your current working tree reflects.

Of course, you want to be able to make changes to the files in your newly created branch. To do that, you have to check out the branch. You do that with the git checkout command like this:

```
prompt> git checkout new
Switched to branch "new"
```

That's all it takes to switch. Run git branch again without any parameters to see that the current branch has changed:

```
prompt> git branch
  master
* new
```

Most of the time when you create a branch, you want to immediately check it out so you can start working with it. Git provides a quick shortcut to do that. You can create a branch and check it out in one step by adding the -b parameter to git checkout.

Let's create another branch using git checkout -b. Each branch has to have a unique name, so you have to choose something besides master or new.

Let's go with alternate to keep it simple:

```
prompt> git checkout -b alternate master
Switched to a new branch "alternate"
```

Notice this time I added a third parameter, master. The extra parameter tells Git to create the branch from the master branch instead of the current branch.

You can provide the extra branch to git branch as well, and it will create the new branch from whatever branch you specify.

Now that you have these branches, you can start making changes that are tracked in that one branch. Next up, we'll cover how to merge those changes between branches.

5.3 Merging Changes Between Branches

These branches are great for organizing your repository, but you need to be able to share changes between branches. This is done through *merging*.

Merging does exactly what it sounds like. It takes two—or sometimes more—branches and merges them into one. There are a couple of different ways to merge changes between branches. This section covers the following:

- *Straight merges* take the history of one branch and the history of the other branch and attempt to merge them together.
- *Squashed commits* take the history of one branch and compress—or "squash"—it into one commit on top of another branch.
- *Cherry-picking* a commit pulls a single commit from a different branch and applies it to the current branch.

Straight Merging

A straight merge takes one branch and merges it into another branch. You can use this when you want to pull the entire history of one branch into another.

Let's demonstrate this by adding some new changes to the alternate branch you just created. Add a new file called about.html, and add some information about yourself.

Once you've created the new file, add and commit it to your repository:

```
prompt> git add about.html
prompt> git commit -m "add the skeleton of an about page"
Created commit 217a88e: add the skeleton of an about page
 1 files changed, 15 insertions(+), 0 deletions(-)
 create mode 100644 about.html
```

Now you have a commit on the alternate branch that doesn't exist on the master branch. You can now use the git merge command to merge the two.

First, you have to start by switching to the branch you want to use as your target for the merge. In this case, that's the master branch:

```
prompt> git checkout master
Switched to branch "master"
```

Next, you can use git merge. In its simplest form, git merge takes the name of the branch you want to merge into your current branch:

```
prompt> git merge alternate
Updating 9a23464..217a88e
Fast forward
 about.html |   15 +++++++++++++++
 1 files changed, 15 insertions(+), 0 deletions(-)
 create mode 100644 about.html
```

Now the changes from the alternate branch are merged into your master branch.

Squashing Commits

Feature branches are a common way to use branches in Git. You create your new feature, or maybe even fix a bug, inside a branch and then create a squashed commit to merge the changes back.

They are "squashed" because Git takes all the history of one branch and compresses it into one commit in the other branch. Be careful with squashed commits. Most of the time you want to keep all the commits separate in your history. If the changes of a branch represent one individual change, then it's a candidate for squashing.

These are helpful when you're creating a new feature or fixing a bug that requires some experimentation. You don't need each commit tracing your experimentation; you just need the final outcome.

You need to have something to merge in order to create a squashed commit. Let's create a branch from the master branch called contact and check it out:

```
prompt> git checkout -b contact master
Switched to a new branch "contact"
```

Now add a file called contact.html. Add your email address to the file, and then commit it.

```
prompt> git add contact.html
prompt> git commit -m "add contact file with email"
Created commit 5b4fc7b: add contact file with email
 1 files changed, 15 insertions(+), 0 deletions(-)
 create mode 100644 contact.html
```

Now add a second email address so there are two ways to contact you, and commit it separately:

```
prompt> git commit -m "add secondary email" -a
Created commit 2f30ccd: add secondary email
 1 files changed, 4 insertions(+), 0 deletions(-)
```

Now you have two commits in your contact branch. You can squash these two commits back into the master branch as one commit.

First, you need to switch back to the master branch:

```
prompt> git checkout master
Switched to branch "master"
```

Now call git merge, and pass it the --squash parameter. Adding the --squash option tells git merge to take all the commits from the other branch and squash them into one commit:

```
prompt> git merge --squash contact
Updating 217a88e..2f30ccd
Fast forward
Squash commit -- not updating HEAD
 contact.html |   19 +++++++++++++++++++
 1 files changed, 19 insertions(+), 0 deletions(-)
 create mode 100644 contact.html
```

Now both of your commits from contact have been applied to your working tree and are staged for a commit, but they have not been committed. You can run git status to see the changes:

```
prompt> git status
# On branch master
# Your branch is ahead of 'origin/master' by 1 commit.
#
# Changes to be committed:
#   (use "git reset HEAD <file>..." to unstage)
#
#       new file:   contact.html
#
```

All that's left now is for you to commit the change like any other commit:

```
prompt> git commit -m "add contact page" \
    -m "has primary and secondary email"
Created commit 18f822e: add contact page
 1 files changed, 19 insertions(+), 0 deletions(-)
 create mode 100644 contact.html
```

Squashing and straight merges both have their uses. Sometimes, you need just one commit, though. Cherry-picking is useful in these cases.

Cherry-Picking Commits

Sometimes you need to merge only one commit between branches and don't need to do a full merge. The full merge might be a bad idea because the branch has features that you can't use yet or other changes that aren't ready for this branch yet.

So, when do you need to pull just one commit? Maybe it's a bug that has been fixed or there's a class that needs to be shared between branches. You can pull those individual commits using git cherry-pick.

Just like the name implies, it "cherry-picks" a commit and adds it to your current branch. Let's run through a quick, albeit contrived, example and create a third commit in your contact branch.

First, you need to make sure you're on the contact branch:

```
prompt> git checkout contact
Switched to branch "contact"
```

Next, now that you've switched, add a new link to another way to contact you, such as your Twitter account, and commit it:

```
prompt> git commit -m "add link to twitter" -a
Created commit 321d76f: add link to twitter
 1 files changed, 4 insertions(+), 0 deletions(-)
```

With the commit name—321d76f—in hand, you can cherry-pick it anywhere. Remember, the commit names are universally unique, so your commit name will be different from the one I created. Let's bring it over to the master branch:

```
prompt> git checkout master
Switched to branch "master"
prompt> git cherry-pick 321d76f
Finished one cherry-pick.
Created commit 294655e: add link to twitter
 1 files changed, 4 insertions(+), 0 deletions(-)
```

Of course, this example isn't too impressive since your contact branch has only that one change, but it does demonstrate the raw steps you need to take to perform a cherry-pick.

Imagine you created a new class in one branch while you're refactoring some existing code—maybe a class that implements a generic pattern such as a registry. It's generic enough that you want to reuse it, but it's stuck in another branch that you can't merge completely because you don't want or need all the functionality in that branch.

You can use git cherry-pick to pick that change out. By default, a new commit is created with the changes from that cherry-picked commit. This is OK in most cases, but what if the code you need is in several commits?

To cherry-pick multiple commits, give git cherry-pick the -n parameter. That tells Git to do the merge but stop before creating a commit. Let's demonstrate.

First, let's remove it with git reset. This command is something you haven't seen yet, but don't worry—we'll cover how to use it in Section 6.6, *Resetting Changes*, on page 85.

```
prompt> git reset --hard HEAD^
HEAD is now at 18f822e add contact page
```

Now that the last commit is removed, you can run git cherry-pick again with the -n parameter:

```
prompt> git cherry-pick -n 321d76f
Finished one cherry-pick.
```

Notice that Git stopped at Finished one cherry-pick this time. You can run git status and see that the new file has been added and is staged and ready for commit:

```
prompt> git status
# On branch master
# Your branch is ahead of 'origin/master' by 2 commits.
#
# Changes to be committed:
#   (use "git reset HEAD <file>..." to unstage)
#
#       modified:   contact.html
#
```

Now you can proceed to cherry-pick another change. You can commit the changes with whatever message you would like once all the commits have been cherry-picked.

Go ahead and commit the change. But don't add a message with -m. The editor will come up with the commit message of the commit you just cherry-picked:

```
prompt> git commit
Created commit 0bb3dfb: add link to twitter
 1 files changed, 4 insertions(+), 0 deletions(-)
```

That covers the basics of merging. So far, our merges have been pretty straightforward and easy, but what happens if there is a problem merging? Handling those conflicts is the subject of the next section.

5.4 Handling Conflicts

What happens when you edit the same file in different ways in two different branches and then try to merge them? Git tries to merge them together, but sometimes it can't.

It is called a *conflict* when Git can't automatically merge the commits together. Conflicts occur most commonly when the same area in a file is changed in different ways in each branch. For example, you might use a different variable name in each branch. Git can't tell which one you want to use, so it stops with a conflict and lets you fix it.

Let's demonstrate how a conflict works. First, let's create a new branch called about to add our work in:

```
prompt> git checkout -b about master
Switched to branch "about"
```

Next, add a list of a few of your favorite programming languages. Save the file, and then add and commit it to the repository:

```
prompt> git add about.html
prompt> git commit -m "a list of my favorite programming languages"
Created commit 01fe684: a list of my favorite programming languages
 1 files changed, 7 insertions(+), 0 deletions(-)
```

Now, create a second branch called about2, but don't switch to it just yet:

```
prompt> git branch about2 about
```

Before you switch branches, add another language to your about.html file, and commit your change:

```
prompt> git commit -m "add Javascript to list" -a
Created commit 9e114ac: add Javascript to list
 1 files changed, 1 insertions(+), 0 deletions(-)
```

Now you have a change that exists in the about branch but not in the about2 branch because we created the branch before we made the second commit.

Switch over to about2. You can refresh about.html to see that the last entry isn't there:

```
prompt> git checkout about2
Switched to branch "about2"
```

Add another name to about.html on the same line where you added your last entry, but this time make it something different.

Once it's saved, commit your new change:

```
prompt> git commit -m "add EMCAScript to list" -a
Created commit b84ffdc: add EMCAScript to list
 1 files changed, 1 insertions(+), 0 deletions(-)
```

Now you manufactured a conflict. Of course, most of the time you won't realize what has happened until later when Git complains as you try to merge. Let's see this in action.

Start by switching back to about, and then try merging about2 into it:

```
prompt> git checkout about
Switched to branch "about"
prompt> git merge about2
Auto-merged about.html
CONFLICT (content): Merge conflict in about.html
Automatic merge failed; fix conflicts and then commit the result.
```

Notice the CONFLICT line. It tells us that there was a conflict in the about.html file.

This is what my list from about.html looks like now:

```
    <ul>
        <li>Erlang</li>
        <li>Python</li>
        <li>Objective C</li>
<<<<<<< HEAD:about.html
        <li>Javascript</li>
=======
        <li>EMCAScript</li>
>>>>>>> about2:about.html
    </ul>
```

You can see that there are two different names in the last <li> element. The first is the commit you made to about earlier. The second is the line you just added to about2. The conflict is prefixed by this:

```
<<<<<<< HEAD:about.html
```

The code that conflicted from the other branch is displayed after the ======= separator and suffixed with the following line:

```
>>>>>>> about2:about.html
```

The prefix and suffix lines tell you two things. First, any code that is preceded by "<<<<<<<" is the code in your current branch, and any code suffixed with ">>>>>>>" is from the other branch. Second, the name of what you are trying to merge is included before the filename. In this case, it is the HEAD—remember, that's the name of the most current commit in your current branch—that conflicts with the about2 branch.

For simple merges, you can edit the file by hand to resolve the conflict. Once you have saved your changes, you need to stage and commit your changes like normal.

For more complex merges, using a visual tool such as kdiff3[2] in Linux or opendiff[3] on OS X is helpful. Git can launch a merging tool by using the git mergetool command.

git mergetool attempts to locate a tool to handle the merge for you. It will sometimes find multiple tools. When it does, it asks which tool you want to use.

```
prompt> git mergetool
Merging the files: about.html

Normal merge conflict for 'about.html':
  {local}: modified
  {remote}: modified
Hit return to start merge resolution tool (opendiff):
```

git mergetool looks at the value of merge.tool in your configuration; then it scans your system for valid merge resolution tools. Valid tools are kdiff3, tkdiff, meld, xxdiff, emerge, vimdiff, gvimdiff, ecmerge, and opendiff.

In the previous session, all I have to do is press the Enter key to start OS X's FileMerge Utility via opendiff. You can see what it looks like in Figure 5.1, on the facing page.

Each tool is a little different, so a step-by-step guide is impossible, but the overall result is the same. Each conflicting change is displayed, and you choose which one you want to use.

Git stages your changes for commit once you successfully resolve the conflicts. Go ahead and commit your change. Leave -m off, and Git will prepopulate your log message with a message describing what just happened:

```
prompt> git commit
Created commit f846762: Merge branch 'about2' into about
```

---

2. http://kdiff3.sourceforge.net
3. opendiff is part of Xcode from Apple that can be downloaded from http://developer.apple.com/tools/.

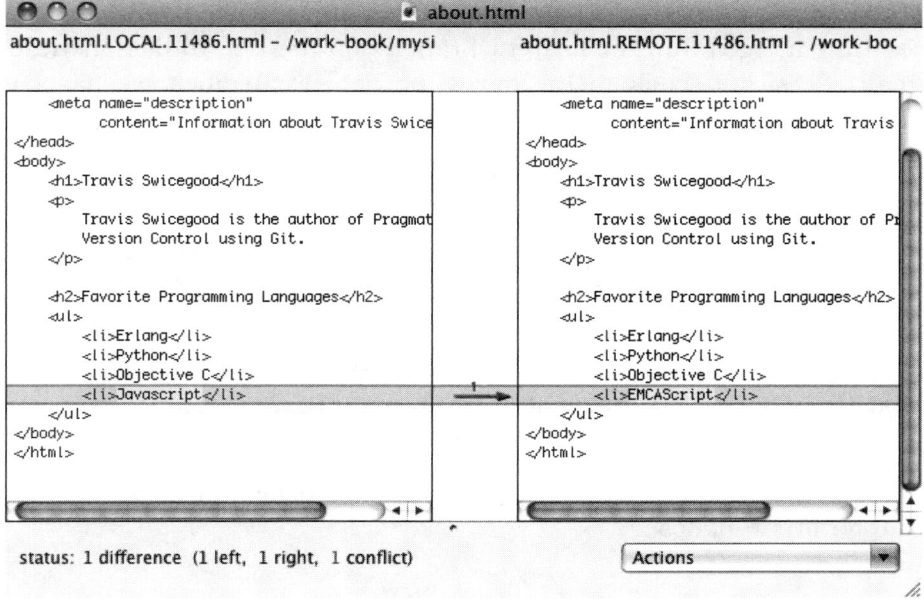

Figure 5.1: OS X'S FILEMERGE UTILITY

That covers the creating and merging branches and shows how to handle the conflicts that inevitably arise. These are three of the areas where most of your time gets spent when working with branches. Up next, we move on to some housecleaning: deleting branches.

5.5 Deleting Branches

Branches can outlive their usefulness. The release was tagged; the experiment was proven successful or failed. When this happens, you should delete the branch to keep your repository's branches from growing out of control.

After you merge your changes back into your current branch, such as the about2 branch you created, you can use the -d parameter on git branch to delete the old branch:

```
prompt> git branch -d about2
Deleted branch about2.
```

This works only when the branch you're trying to delete has been successfully merged into the current branch you are on. To demonstrate this, let's switch back to the master branch. Remember, we haven't merged any of our changes from the about branch yet.

```
prompt> git checkout master
Switched to branch "master"
prompt> git branch -d about
error: The branch 'about' is not an ancestor of your current HEAD.
If you are sure you want to delete it, run 'git branch -D about'.
```

Now, if you are sure you want to remove the about branch without merging, you can force it to be removed by swapping out the -d for a -D. That tells Git not to check and to make sure that the branch you are trying to delete has been merged into the current branch.

Let's revisit renaming branches one last time before we wrap up this chapter on branches.

5.6 Renaming Branches

Branch names serve as a reminder as to what you're working with. Sometimes those reminders need to change. Sometimes you need to fix a typo.

Let's take our contact branch. There was one method of contact when it started, but now there's three. Let's rename it to contacts:

```
prompt> git branch -m contact contacts
prompt> git branch
  about
  alternate
  contacts
* master
  new
```

The -m parameter will not overwrite an existing branch, so the new branch—the second branch name you provide—must be unique. Git complains like this if you try to rename a branch using an existing name:

```
prompt> git branch -m master contacts
fatal: A branch named 'contacts' already exists.
```

You can override this behavior by changing the -m option to the -M option. The uppercase *M* tells Git to force an overwrite if the other branch exists. Use this with care.

That wraps up our tour of branches. We've covered the mechanics of creating and maintaining branches. Understanding how branches fit into Git is fundamental to being efficient with Git.

So far, we've covered how to use Git moving forward, but a key part of any VCS is how we can use it to see where we've been. The next chapter Chapter 6, *Working with Git's History*, on page 71 deals with that.

Those who cannot remember the past are condemned to repeat it.

► George Santayana

Chapter 6

Working with Git's History

A key aspect of any version control system is its history. Every new file you add and every change you add creates one more commit in its history.

In this chapter, you'll learn how to do the following:

- Inspect the history of your repository using `git log`
- Specify ranges of commits to help searching
- View differences between commits
- Annotate files with a line-by-line history
- Follow content as you move it around
- Undo changes you've made
- Rewrite the history of your repository

Inspecting that history can provide invaluable information. "Why does this file not conform to our coding standard?" A quick check of a file's log might show that it has not been touched since it was originally hacked together with a log message of `make ready for client demo`.

If your questions are more specific, Git can show you an annotated version of your file that tells you who changed each line and when. You can drill down further to show the differences between two revisions of a file.

Finally, Git lets you rewrite the history of your repository in several ways, but be careful, or the other members on your team might quit talking to you after they spend a morning trying to fix broken merges.

In this chapter, you'll learn how to deal with all these tasks; we'll start with looking at where we've been by learning about git log.

This chapter uses the repository you've been working on throughout the book. If you don't have a copy and want to follow along with the examples in this chapter, you can clone the repository from GitHub:

```
prompt> git clone git://github.com/tswicegood/mysite-chp5.git
Initialized empty Git repository in /work/mysite-chp5/.git/
remote: Counting objects: 41, done.
remote: Compressing objects: 100% (35/35), done.
remote: Total 41 (delta 14), reused 0 (delta 0)
Receiving objects: 100% (41/41), 4.52 KiB, done.
Resolving deltas: 100% (14/14), done.
prompt> cd mysite-chp5
```

6.1 Inspecting Git's Log

The commit log is the most common way for you to inspect what has happened to your repository. Git shows each new commit's log entry, along with who made the commit, when, and optionally the changes that were made.

It's displayed in a reverse-chronological order, like a blog. You can provide all sorts of parameters to filter the log, but let's start with the basics. Just type git log at the command prompt from within your working tree:

```
prompt> git log
commit 0bb3dfb752fa3c890ffc781fd6bd5dc5d34cd3be
Author: Travis Swicegood <development@domain51.com>
Date:   Sat Oct 4 11:06:47 2008 -0500

    add link to twitter

commit 18f822eb1044761f59aebaf7739261042ae10392
Author: Travis Swicegood <development@domain51.com>
Date:   Sat Oct 4 10:34:51 2008 -0500

    add contact page

    has primary and secondary email
:
```

Git sends the log output through less if there is more than it can display on one screen. That lets you scroll through the log. You can tell that there's more output by the presence of the : at the bottom of the screen.

The default output from git log shows you four pieces of information about each commit: the commit name, the author, the date, and the log message. The first three are on the first three lines. The rest of the entry until the next line beginning with commit is the log entry.

Sometimes our log messages aren't as descriptive as we thought they were when we view them six months later. Often, viewing the code that changed in conjunction with the log message can help jog our memories. Adding the -p option tells Git to display the diff that revision created.

Often you need to view only a set number of commits. You can add -1 to the log command to limit the log to one commit, -2 to limit it to two commits, and so on. For example, git log -10 shows the last ten log entries.

You can view the log starting at a given revision by passing the revision as an option at the command line:

```
prompt> git log 7b1558c
commit 7b1558c92a7f755d8343352d5051384d98f104e4
Author: Travis Swicegood <development@domain51.com>
Date:   Sun Sep 21 14:20:21 2008 -0500

    add in hello world HTML
```

Note that I used a short commit name—the first seven characters of the commit name. Git tries to match any hash you provide it, but it has to be unique. Four or five characters normally matches, but seven or eight is almost guaranteed to be unique.

Now that you have the basics down with git log, it's time to dive into more complex ways of telling Git what commit—or commits—you're looking for.

6.2 Specifying Revision Ranges

I have what I've come to call a "nonhistorian" brain. Specifics take a lot of work for me to remember. I know the gist of American history, but I can't tell you specific dates unless they ended up spawning a national holiday.

The same thing happens when I code: "I added that functionality last Monday or Tuesday." "I fixed that bug this morning." Git has a lot of functionality for looking through its logs that way.

Git provides some other useful ways for filtering the commits that you see. Say you want to look at commits only from the last five hours, so you add --since="5 hours". Your command now looks like this:

```
prompt> git log --since="5 hours"
commit 0bb3dfb752fa3c890ffc781fd6bd5dc5d34cd3be
Author: Travis Swicegood <development@domain51.com>
Date:   Sat Oct 4 11:06:47 2008 -0500

    add link to twitter
```

Likewise, you can skip the last five hours and view only those commits older than that by using --before="5 hours":

```
prompt> git log --before="5 hours" -1
commit 18f822eb1044761f59aebaf7739261042ae10392
Author: Travis Swicegood <development@domain51.com>
Date:   Sat Oct 4 10:34:51 2008 -0500

    add contact page

    has primary and secondary email
```

The --since and --before options can take most English ways of specifying a date. Git can understand --since="24 hours", --since="1 minute", and --before="2008-10.01"—yes, it is smart enough to parse that date, even with the mixed hyphen and period.

You can also pass ranges of commits in by separating two revisions with oldest-revision..newest-revision. You should always specify the oldest revision first so Git can understand what you want:

```
prompt> git log 18f822e..0bb3dfb
commit 0bb3dfb752fa3c890ffc781fd6bd5dc5d34cd3be
Author: Travis Swicegood <development@domain51.com>
Date:   Sat Oct 4 11:06:47 2008 -0500

    add link to twitter
```

At first glance, that output looks wrong. We told it to show us the log from revision 18f822e to revision 0bb3dfb. The first time I used a command similar to this, I thought it would include 18f822e, but Git doesn't. Instead, Git interprets that range to mean every commit *after* 18f822e to 5ef8.

HEAD is synonymous with the latest revision of the current branch in your repository. In our earlier command, we could swap out 0bb3dfb with HEAD and get the same result.

```
prompt> git log 18f822e..HEAD
commit 0bb3dfb752fa3c890ffc781fd6bd5dc5d34cd3be
Author: Travis Swicegood <development@domain51.com>
Date:   Sat Oct 4 11:06:47 2008 -0500

    add link to twitter
```

You can drop the final HEAD from that range because Git assumes HEAD is what you mean if you leave the last value blank:

```
prompt> git log 18f822e..
commit 0bb3dfb752fa3c890ffc781fd6bd5dc5d34cd3be
Author: Travis Swicegood <development@domain51.com>
Date:   Sat Oct 4 11:06:47 2008 -0500

    add link to twitter
```

With ranges, you can swap out the commit name for a tag name too. This is useful for seeing what has changed since a particular tag and for looking at the revision history between two tags.

```
prompt> git log --pretty=format:"%h %s" 1.0..HEAD
0bb3dfb add link to twitter
18f822e add contact page
217a88e add the skeleton of an about page
9a23464 rename to more appropriate name
6f1bf6f Change biography link and add contact link
4333289 add in a bio link
```

Notice that this time I added the --pretty parameter to git log. The format:"%h %s" option tells Git to display short hashes and the first line of the commit log, which is the subject.

A more common usage is --pretty=oneline, but the output from it is too wide to fit on this page. There's a bunch of different formats you can use. The git log manual page lists them all. If your git log command with ranges doesn't generate anything, make sure it's a range that can actually work. Remember, the oldest revision has to be specified first. If you don't do that, Git won't complain; it just won't show you anything.

Another common way to specify a revision is by its relationship to another revision. There are two operators you can use:

- ^: A caret acts like a minus one. 18f822e^ translates into the revision that comes before the revision that matches 18f822e. You can also use multiple carets: 18f822e^^ is two revisions prior to 18f822e, and so on. On Windows you need to add quotation marks around your revision if it as a caret in it. 18f822e^ should be "18f822e^", otherwise Windows can't process your command properly.

- ~N: The tilde and a number operator subtracts N from the commit name. Using the last examples, 18f822e~1 is the revision prior to 18f822e, and 18f822e~2 is two revisions prior to 18f822e.

You can mix and match these two operators. The following three commands would all grab the same revision:

```
prompt> git log -1 HEAD^^^
... log entry ...
prompt> git log -1 HEAD^~2
... log entry ...
prompt> git log -1 HEAD~1^^
... log entry ...
prompt> git log -1 HEAD~3
... log entry ...
```

You can also use revisions with carets or tildes in the ranges we talked about earlier. So, you can do the following:

```
prompt> git log HEAD~10..HEAD
fatal: ambiguous argument 'HEAD~10..HEAD': unknown revision or path
not in the working tree.
Use '--' to separate paths from revisions
```

Oops. That's what happens when you specify a revision that does not exist. You get the "unknown revision" error. Now that we have all the revisions ranges and filters down, let's look at viewing differences between a file at different points in history.

6.3 Looking at Differences Between Versions

In Section 4.3, *Seeing What Has Changed*, on page 48, you learned how to use git diff to look at the differences between your working copy and the repository. You can also use it to view the history within the repository:

```
prompt> git diff 18f822e
diff --git a/contact.html b/contact.html
index 64135cb..63617c2 100644
--- a/contact.html
+++ b/contact.html
@@ -13,6 +13,10 @@
     <p>
         <a href="mailto:tswicegood@gmail.com">Gmail</a>
     </p>
+
+    <p>
+        <a href="http://twitter.com/tswicegood">Twitter</a>
+    </p>
 </body>
 </html>
```

All the revision ranges and modifiers are the same as git log. The only difference is that Git shows you all the changes mashed together instead of incrementally.

Using git diff with tags is a great way to get statistics between releases. With it, you can figure out how many lines of code were changed and how many were removed.

There's another cool option for git diff that prints some statistics about the changes that have been made. Just add the --stat option:

```
prompt> git diff --stat 1.0
 about.html    |   15 +++++++++++++++
 contact.html  |   23 +++++++++++++++++++++++
 hello.html    |   13 +++++++++++++
 index.html    |    9 ---------
 4 files changed, 51 insertions(+), 9 deletions(-)
```

This is a great way to see the amount of code that has been touched in the last week or since the last tag.

Notice that I gave it a tag. Git assumes you want to compare against the HEAD if you don't give it a second revision.

Now that you know how the log works and how to show differences between different revisions of the file, let's look at the history line-by-line.

6.4 Finding Out Who's to Blame

You're looking at a file in your project, and one block of code—it might be one line or ten—looks out of place. Or maybe there's a set of nested conditions that you're trying to wrap your head around so you can refactor it to make it more understandable.

Looking at the log of a file and differences between revisions can be helpful, but there's a more useful command when you need information about a particular block of code. git blame prefixes every line with the commit name, committer, and timestamp.

Here are the first two lines of git blame output on hello.html with my last name shortened so the output fits on the page:

```
prompt> git blame hello.html
^7b1558c index.html (Travis S. 2008-09-21 14:20:21 -0500  1) <html>
a5dacabd index.html (Travis S. 2008-09-21 20:37:47 -0500  2) <head>
```

There's a couple of interesting pieces of information here. First, the first eight characters on each line show the commit hash. Notice that the first line has a ^ before it. That signifies that it's the first commit to the repository.

Next, notice that the filename index.html is listed. Remember when you created this file? It was originally named index.html. That second column, if it's present, is Git's way of telling that this change was originally in another file. After that, it displays the committer's name and the time the commit was created. It's followed with the line number and then the line of code.

Of course, you rarely need to see the entire file annotated. Git makes it easy to annotate a portion of a file with its -L option. This tells Git to display only a certain set of line ranges. It takes single parameter—a <start>,<end>.

The start and end can be numbers. For example, the following loads the blame for lines 12 and 13 of the hello.html file:

```
prompt> git blame -L 12,13 hello.html
^7b1558c index.html (Travis S. 2008-09-21 14:20:21 -0500 12) </body>
^7b1558c index.html (Travis S. 2008-09-21 14:20:21 -0500 13) </html>
```

The ending number doesn't have to be a specific number. You can specify it as +N or -N to specify a range. This generates the same output as the previous command:

```
prompt> git blame -L 12,+2 hello.html
^7b1558c index.html (Travis S. 2008-09-21 14:20:21 -0500 12) </body>
^7b1558c index.html (Travis S. 2008-09-21 14:20:21 -0500 13) </html>
```

Using the -N notation allows you to subtract that many lines. You can use -L 12,-2 to show lines 12 and 11 of your file:

```
prompt> git blame -L 12,-2 hello.html
4333289e index.html (Travis S. 2008-09-22 07:54:28 -0500 11)     </ul>
^7b1558c index.html (Travis S. 2008-09-21 14:20:21 -0500 12) </body>
```

Using numbers is often convenient. A lot of the time you have an editor open with the line numbers displayed when you need to figure out what's going on in a file, but Git provides another way to specify the start and end—regular expressions.[1]

1. Git uses POSIX regular expressions if you're curious about what type of regular expression you can use.

Many books[2] have been written on regular expressions, so I won't cover them here other than to show you an example. You can write the blame command we've used previously using a regular expression like this:

```
prompt> git blame -L "/<\/body>/",+2 hello.html
^7b1558c index.html (Travis S. 2008-09-21 14:20:21 -0500 12) </body>
^7b1558c index.html (Travis S. 2008-09-21 14:20:21 -0500 13) </html>
```

Of course, a lot of times the output from blame isn't going to be helpful. Perhaps the coding standard changed and someone was performing some cleanup. You can use any of the methods we talked about in Section 6.2, *Specifying Revision Ranges*, on page 73 to specify where you want to look. For example, if you want to look at the hello.html file before the 4333289e commit, you can use this command:

```
prompt> git blame -L "/<\/body>/",-2 4333289e^ -- hello.html
fatal: no such path hello.html in 4333289e^
```

Oh, that's right, hello.html didn't exist at commit 4333289e^. It was still index.html at that point. Run the command again with index.html as the filename. Notice that there's a -- between the end of the options and the actual filename. That tells Git that you're specifying a file.

```
prompt> git blame -L "/<\/body>/",-2 4333289e^ -- index.html
^7b1558c (Travis Swicegood 2008-09-21 14:20:21 -0500 7)   <h1>Hello...
^7b1558c (Travis Swicegood 2008-09-21 14:20:21 -0500 8) </body>
```

That covers the basics of git blame. You've seen it display when files have moved, but it can also follow changes from copy and pasting. You'll learn how to do that next.

6.5 Following Content

As we talked about in Section 4.4, *Copying Files—or Not*, on page 52, Git can track when the content moves within a file and even when it moves to another file. This is useful when you're trying to track down the original commit and author of a few lines of code.

To keep from matching lines like a closing bracket in C or a simple constructor in Python, Git tries to match at least three lines when it tries to detect a copy and paste.

Let's create a new file to demonstrate this functionality.

2. *Mastering Regular Expressions* [Fri97] is one such excellent book.

Call it original.txt, and put the following three lines in it:

```
This is the first line.
This happens to be the second line.
And this, it is the third and final line.
```

Once you've saved your new file, add it to the repository, and commit:

```
prompt> git add original.txt
prompt> git commit -m "commit of original text file"
Created commit b87524b: commit of original text file
 1 files changed, 3 insertions(+), 0 deletions(-)
 create mode 100644 original.txt
```

Now, let's edit that file and duplicate the entire file. Just copy and paste the first three lines onto the next three lines, and save it. Running git diff from the command line shows output similar to this:

```
prompt> git diff
diff --git a/original.txt b/original.txt
index 4d9f742..350f1bb 100644
--- a/original.txt
+++ b/original.txt
@@ -1,3 +1,6 @@
 This is the first line.
 This happens to be the second line.
 And this, it is the third and final line.
+This is the first line.
+This happens to be the second line.
+And this, it is the third and final line.
```

Commit this change so Git knows about it. Now we can utilize the git blame command to view the history of each line of the file:

```
1 prompt> git blame original.txt
2 b87524b7 (... 1) This is the first line.
3 b87524b7 (... 2) This happens to be the second line.
4 b87524b7 (... 3) And this, it is the third and final line.
5 222cb821 (... 4) This is the first line.
6 222cb821 (... 5) This happens to be the second line.
7 222cb821 (... 6) And this, it is the third and final line.
```

Your output will have more information displayed. The ... in this output is my name along with the timestamp of the commit, but I had to remove it to fit it on the page.

The first eight characters you'll recognize as a short name. The number before the content shows the line of text that is being displayed. Lines 2 to 4 of the previous session, lines 1 to 3 of the file, all have the same commit name, and lines 5 to 7 have another. These signify the two commits that we've made so far.

Now let's rerun the command, but this time add the -M parameter. This tells git blame to detect lines that have moved or been copied around within the same file:

```
prompt> git blame -M original.txt
b87524b7 (... 1) This is the first line.
b87524b7 (... 2) This happens to be the second line.
b87524b7 (... 3) And this, it is the third and final line.
b87524b7 (... 4) This is the first line.
b87524b7 (... 5) This happens to be the second line.
b87524b7 (... 6) And this, it is the third and final line.
```

Now all the commit names are the same. Because Git tracks content, it realizes that it has more of the same content when it detects the repeating pattern.

Git can also track copies between files. Let's copy the original.txt file into a new file with an equally original name: copy.txt.

Now add and commit this file. Now add -C -C to git blame to see the copy between files:

```
prompt> git blame -C -C copy.txt
b87524b7 original.txt (... 1) This is the first line.
b87524b7 original.txt (... 2) This happens to be the second line.
b87524b7 original.txt (... 3) And this, it is the third and final line.
b87524b7 original.txt (... 4) This is the first line.
b87524b7 original.txt (... 5) This happens to be the second line.
b87524b7 original.txt (... 6) And this, it is the third and final line.
```

Git displays not only the original commit name, b87524b7, but also the original filename, original.txt. git log can also show us when whole files have been copied when we pass it the same -C -C parameter.

When detecting for copies within the git log command, we also have to pass the -p parameter. It tells Git to display the changes from each commit in addition to the normal log information.

```
prompt> git log -C -C -1 -p
commit 540ecb73f652a882ad235c85b61ffb657d3d4969
Author: Travis Swicegood <development@domain51.com>
Date:   Sat Oct 4 17:08:16 2008 -0500

    copy original to show cross-file blame

diff --git a/original.txt b/copy.txt
similarity index 100%
copy from original.txt
copy to copy.txt
```

We can see that Git tells us that the copy.txt file is a 100 percent match for original.txt.

Now that we've covered the basics of change history, it's time to bring out the inner revisionist historian in yourself and start thinking about revising the history of your repository.

6.6 Undoing Changes

Hindsight is 20/20, or so they say. Working with your code is no exception. You commit a change and then realize it had a password in it that you shouldn't be sharing.

In a centralized repository where every change is sent back to a main repository, you are almost out of luck. There are some hoops you can jump through if you have administrator access, but it might well corrupt data.

Git plans for this type of mistake, however. All your changes happen locally and are shared only when you push them to a public repository. Since you're the only one who has to stay in sync, you can rewrite your history as much as you want!

Dangers of Rewriting History

Before we start, a word of caution: be careful how you use the commands in this section if you use Git like you would a centralized repository and push every commit back upstream. Changing the history after you've shared it can lead to major headaches when others try to sync against your changes.

All these commands except git revert—which is covered in Section 6.6, *Reverting Commits*, on page 84—change the history of your repository. This is dangerous in a centralized repository. How can the repository keep track of content when its commits move around, are renamed, or even disappear?

One of the values of completely distributed development is that you share only what is ready. Make sure changes are ready before you push them. By keeping all your changes local until they are ready, you leave yourself the option of rewriting your repository's history without worrying how it affects others.

Once you push your changes, you lose some of that flexibility—well, only if you want to keep everyone else on your team talking to you.

When you push changes, then change your history, and push those changes that are different, you can cause problems for people who already have the first set of changes you published. For more information on pushing changes, see Section 7.4, *Pushing Changes*, on page 96.

Now that we've covered the dangers in what we're about do to, let's get to the good stuff. Up first, amending commits.

Amending Commits

We've all been there. You're writing code in a new, still sort of unfamiliar language and forget a full stop at the end of a line or leave off a semicolon.[3]

Correcting these small problems with Git is simple. Make the correction, stage the change, and add --amend when you commit.

To demonstrate, add a link to your blog or a website you frequent in your contact.html file, except put a typo in it:

```
prompt> git commit -m "add link to blog" -a
Created commit c3531c4: add link to blog
 1 files changed, 4 insertions(+), 0 deletions(-)
```

Now, fix the URL and commit the changes again, except add --amend to the commit command:

```
prompt> git commit -C HEAD -a --amend
Created commit 45eaf98: add link to blog
 1 files changed, 4 insertions(+), 0 deletions(-)
```

That command introduces a new option to git commit, -C. This option tells Git to use the log message from the commit specified—in this case HEAD, but it could have been any valid commit name as well—instead of explicitly providing a new message. You use the parameter in its lowercase form, -c, to tell Git to launch the editor with the message already filled in so you tweak it before finalizing the commit.

Amending a commit should be done only when you are working with the last commit. If you made a mistake and need to correct it after other commits have been made, you want to use git revert, which is up next.

---

3. Ironically, I had to use --amend when writing this section of the book because I had a typo in one of the tags and didn't catch it until after I had committed.

Reverting Commits

Sometimes code doesn't work out. It requires a certain architecture or introduces a new third-party software dependency that the rest of the team isn't on board with. If you've committed your changes already, you need to undo the commits with the new change, or *revert* them.

The simplest way to revert an existing commit is the git revert command. It "reverts" a commit by creating a new commit in your repository that reverses all the changes made by the original commit.

Normally Git commits the reversal immediately, but you can add the -n parameter to tell Git not to commit. This is useful when you need to revert multiple commits. Just run multiple git revert commands with the -n parameter, and Git stages all the changes and waits for you to commit them.

You must provide it with a commit name so it knows what to revert. For example, if you wanted to revert the commit 540ecb7 and HEAD, use the following. Always revert backward—the most recent first. That makes sure you don't have any unnecessary conflicts to work through when reverting multiple commits.

```
prompt> git revert -n HEAD
Finished one revert.
prompt> git revert -n 540ecb7
Removed copy.txt
Finished one revert.
prompt> git commit -m "revert 45eaf98 and 540ecb7"
Created commit 2b3c1de: revert 45eaf98 and 540ecb7
 2 files changed, 0 insertions(+), 10 deletions(-)
 delete mode 100644 copy.txt
```

By default, git revert starts up your editor for your commit message. The default message is added to the editor: Revert "your original log message" followed by the text This reverts commit <commit name>. You can add --no-edit to git revert when you want it to use the default message.

Just like any other commit, make sure you explain why you're making this commit. Just marking that you're reverting a change, like I did here, doesn't say much.

Did it not work? Was it too slow? Say that. You'll thank yourself in six months when you're trying to remember why you reverted that change.

Resetting Changes

Right as you hit the Enter key, you realize you've just committed a configuration file with your private password in it. We've all been there. With a centralized VCS, you have to ask the systems administrator to perform some magic to remove all traces of the commit.

Git assumes we make mistakes like this and allows us to reset the repository to the state we want. git reset takes a commit name as its parameter. It defaults to HEAD if you don't provide one.

You can use the ^ and ~# commit name modifiers to specify a revision. HEAD^ would reset two commits, while 540ecb7~3 would reset to three commits before 540ecb7.

git reset updates the repository and stages the changes for you to commit. This is useful when you notice an error in your previous commit and want to fix it.

Add --soft when you want to stage all the previous commits but not commit them. This gives you a chance to modify the previous commit by adding to or taking away from it.

The final option is --hard, and it should be used with care. It removes the commit from your repository and from your working tree. It's the equivalent of a delete button on your repository with no "undo."

Let's demonstrate this really quickly. That last commit that reverted those two files isn't necessary. So, let's undo it:

```
prompt> git reset --hard HEAD^
HEAD is now at 45eaf98 add link to blog
```

That resets your repository back to the commit before HEAD. It's like that commit that reverted the two files never happened.

6.7 Rewriting History

Revisionist historians view history as a living thing—something that needs to be reevaluated from time to time to make sure the assumptions that were made in the past still apply.

Looking over your code as part of a formal code review is a great way to make sure the assumptions you made last week or last month still apply. Git lets you take this a step further, though, by allowing you to not only review the history of your code but to rewrite it.

There are a few instances where this is useful:

- *Reorder the history so it makes more sense*: This is the hardest to quantify, but you'll know it when you see it. One commit, or maybe more, seems out of place and logically fits in a different order.
- *Squash several commits into one commit*: You realize after the fact that multiple commits should actually be in one big commit because they all relate to the same issue.
- *Break one commit into multiple commits*: This is the reverse of squashing. After looking through the changes, you realize that one commit has multiple changes in it that you want to have as individual commits.

If you're coming from a traditional VCS such as Subversion or CVS, that list might seem like voodoo. The idea of changing a commit after the fact can take getting used to, but actually reordering commits, breaking one commit into multiple commits? That's too much.

That's the power of having a private repository that's not connected with other developers, though. If you share your changes instantly, like all centralized VCS such as Subversion or CVS do, you can't make any changes without risking unresolvable conflicts when someone tries to update with a repository that has changed.

The tool for this kind of voodoo is the interactive mode of Git's rebase command, git rebase -i. Using it, you can craft the history. Here's the last three commits to the repository:

```
prompt> git log --pretty=format:"%h %s" HEAD~3..
45eaf98 add link to blog
540ecb7 copy original to show cross-file blame
222cb82 adding copied lines to showcase git blame
```

In the next section, you'll learn how to move the 45eaf98 commit to the beginning.

Reordering Commits

git rebase in interactive mode is the tool to use to rewrite history. Launching interactive mode starts your editor for you to make the changes you want. You'll remember how Git looks for an editor from Section 4.2, *Committing Changes*, on page 45. You have to provide the rebase command with the revision you want to work from.

In this case, we want HEAD~3:

```
prompt> git rebase -i HEAD~3
... launches configured editor ...
pick 222cb82 adding copied lines to showcase git blame
pick 540ecb7 copy original to show cross-file blame
pick 45eaf98 add link to blog

# Rebase b87524b..45eaf98 onto b87524b
#
# Commands:
#  p, pick = use commit
#  e, edit = use commit, but stop for amending
#  s, squash = use commit, but meld into previous commit
#
# If you remove a line here THAT COMMIT WILL BE LOST.
# However, if you remove everything, the rebase will be aborted.
#
~
~
```

Everything in the editor that begins with a # is a comment and is ignored by Git. The first three lines are the three commits we're working with. Move the pick 45eaf98 line to the top line. Now the first three lines look like this:

```
pick 45eaf98 add link to blog
pick 222cb82 adding copied lines to showcase git blame
pick 540ecb7 copy original to show cross-file blame
```

Save the editor's contents and exit; then Git starts the rebase operation. When it's finished, you can rerun the git log command to see the new order:

```
prompt> git log --pretty=format:"%h %s" HEAD~3..
8c764d3 copy original to show cross-file blame
be53bab adding copied lines to showcase git blame
4f7621d add link to blog
```

Squashing Multiple Commits into One

There is one more thing you can do here. The blog and Twitter commits can be squashed together. So, let's start another rebase, this time against the commit before the Twitter link commit 0bb3dfb^:

```
prompt> git rebase -i 0bb3dfb^
... launched configured editor ...
pick 0bb3dfb add link to twitter
pick b87524b commit of original text file
pick 4f7621d add link to blog
pick be53bab adding copied lines to showcase git blame
pick 8c764d3 copy original to show cross-file blame
```

```
# Rebase 18f822e..8c764d3 onto 18f822e
#
# Commands:
#  p, pick = use commit
#  e, edit = use commit, but stop for amending
#  s, squash = use commit, but meld into previous commit
#
# If you remove a line here THAT COMMIT WILL BE LOST.
# However, if you remove everything, the rebase will be aborted.
#
~
~
```

This time, move pick 4f7621d to come after pick 0bb3dfb, and change pick in the moved line to squash. After you're done, the first five lines should look like this:

```
pick 0bb3dfb add link to twitter
squash 4f7621d add link to blog
pick b87524b commit of original text file
pick be53bab adding copied lines to showcase git blame
pick 8c764d3 copy original to show cross-file blame
```

Save and exit again. After the rebase starts, the editor will come back up and ask you for a commit message for the two commits you're squashing together. The default message looks like this:

```
This is a combination of two commits.
# The first commit's message is:

add link to twitter

# This is the 2nd commit message:

add link to blog
```

You can combine it to say what you like and then save and exit so Git can finish the rebase operation. You can see the new history with another call to git log:

```
prompt> git log --pretty=format:"%h %s" HEAD~4..
7509494 copy original to show cross-file blame
8184d47 adding copied lines to showcase git blame
9a750b3 commit of original text file
b02376d add link to twitter and blog
```

Now, let's undo those changes by breaking b02376d back into two commits.

Breaking One Commit into Multiple Commits

You just reordered a commit and squashed two commits into one. Breaking one commit into two is a little more involved, but it starts out the same way.

Call git rebase -i again. Once the editor launches, edit its contents to look like this:

```
prompt> git rebase -i HEAD~4
... launches editor ...
edit b02376d add link to twitter and blog
pick 9a750b3 commit of original text file
pick 8184d47 adding copied lines to showcase git blame
pick 7509494 copy original to show cross-file blame
```

Notice that the first line says edit now. Save and exit to start the rebase. When Git gets to the commit you told it to edit, it stops and prints the following:

```
Stopped at b02376d... add link to twitter and blog
You can amend the commit now, with

    git commit --amend

Once you are satisfied with your changes, run

    git rebase --continue
```

Running git log -1 shows you that the last commit is the commit you squashed together in the previous section—the commit you told it to edit:

```
prompt> git log -1
commit b02376dbbb76c356d9d44cf65163293db9147d9a
Author: Travis Swicegood <development@domain51.com>
Date:   Sat Oct 4 11:06:47 2008 -0500

    add link to twitter and blog
```

The rebase is paused now, waiting for you to edit the repository. Now you can break that commit apart by using git reset to undo the last commit and then creating two individual commits:

```
prompt> git reset HEAD^
contact.html: locally modified
prompt> git diff
diff --git a/contact.html b/contact.html
index 64135cb..c6cffa7 100644
--- a/contact.html
+++ b/contact.html
@@ -13,6 +13,14 @@
```

```
     <p>
         <a href="mailto:tswicegood@gmail.com">Gmail</a>
     </p>
+
+    <p>
+        <a href="http://twitter.com/tswicegood">Twitter</a>
+    </p>
+
+    <p>
+        <a href="http://www.travisswicegood.com/">Blog</a>
+    </p>
 </body>
 </html>
```

git diff shows all the changes waiting for you to commit. Pull that second link out, and save the contact.html file. With just the link to Twitter, commit your change:

```
prompt> git commit -m "add link to Twitter" -a
Created commit 07950f4: add link to Twitter
 1 files changed, 4 insertions(+), 0 deletions(-)
```

Now, add that link to the blog back in, and create a new commit for it:

```
prompt> git commit -m "add link to blog" -a
Created commit 6c0eebe: add link to blog
 1 files changed, 4 insertions(+), 0 deletions(-)
```

You're finished with the changes—breaking the commit into two—so call git rebase --continue:

```
prompt> git rebase --continue
Successfully rebased and updated refs/heads/master.
```

A quick check of the log shows that there are now two commits back where the squashed commit was.

Of course, this wouldn't be Git if git rebase couldn't serve another function too. It works with branches to keep them synced and move them around. We'll talk about that functionality in Section 9.3, *Rebasing a Branch*, on page 118.

Now you've seen how to work with the history—and sometimes even rewrite it—in Git. These are extremely useful parts of Git, but they aren't things you'll be using every day. At least at first.

As you get more comfortable with concepts like rebasing your repository, you'll find more and more instances where you can use it.

So far we've talked only about working with your local repository. As you'll see in the next chapter, working with remote repositories lets you share your work with others and get updates from them.

Chapter 7

Working with Remote Repositories

Now we've covered everything you need to work on your own. However, the *distributed* in distributed version control means you'll normally be working with other people on your projects.

This chapter is about how to interact with projects on remote repositories. You'll learn the following:

- What the different types of remote repositories are
- How to create a copy of a remote repository
- How to stay up-to-date with remote changes
- How to share your changes by pushing to a remote repository
- How to work with remote branches
- How to add new remote repositories

I'm going to deviate for a minute. Instead of having cloning instructions up front, I've added the instructions in Section 7.2, *Cloning a Remote Repository*, on page 94. Before we dive into working with remote Git repositories, let's talk a little bit about the different networking options you have to connect to different repositories.

7.1 Network Protocols

Git communicates with remote repositories over a network. That network can be your internal LAN, a VPN, or the Internet. Git provides three protocols for communicating with remote repositories:

- SSH
- git
- HTTP/HTTPS

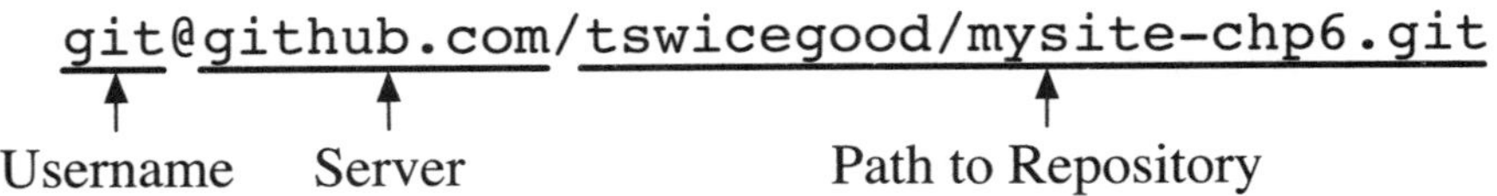

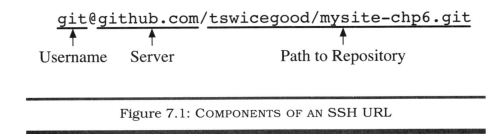

Figure 7.1: COMPONENTS OF AN SSH URL

SSH

Accessing a repository over Secure Shell (SSH) is similar to accessing a repository directly from the file system with one exception. Before the path to the repository, you add the domain name, and username if needed, for the remote repository.

The only difference between the SSH URL (shown in Figure 7.1) and the basic file system URL is the addition of git@github.com. That tells Git to attempt to log on to the github.com server via SSH with the username git and then clone the repository located at the tswicegood/mysite-chp6.git path.

The username, the git@ in the previous example, is optional. You don't have to specify the username when you use the same username on your local computer as you do on the remote server.

In a lot of instances, you share a user with other members on your team to log into the server, and the remote server checks the credentials you provide to make sure you have access to it.

git

Git has its own protocol that has been designed for speed. It is the fastest protocol, but it might run into issues with strict firewalls since it uses port 9418, a port that doesn't normally have network traffic.

In Figure 7.2, on the next page, you can see what a repository URL over the git protocol looks like. git:// specifies the protocol, followed by the server, github.com, followed by the repository name.

In this example, the full path is not specified. When you start a Git server, you tell it what directory to look in for repositories to serve. All that clients have to do is specify the name of the repository they want to access.

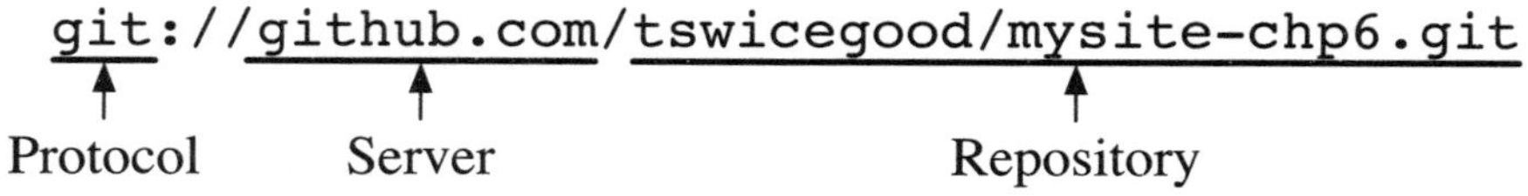

Figure 7.2: COMPONENTS OF A GIT URL

The major difference between this protocol and SSH, besides encryption, is that it is anonymous. This is good if you want to provide public read-only access to your repository, but it can be dangerous if you open it up for writing—you don't want just anyone changing your repository. Almost every time you see a repository using git://, it will be read-only.

It is common for repositories to utilize this protocol to allow other developers to pull their changes while using SSH to push their own changes into the repository to share.

HTTP/HTTPS

The HTTP protocol is generally considered the protocol of last resort. It is the least efficient way to pull changes and requires much more network overhead, but it is almost always allowed by the strictest firewalls and is relatively quick and easy to set up.

Continuing with the example of mysite-chp6.git on the github.com server, if GitHub had HTTP access to its repositories, you would access GitHub with a URL like this:

```
http://github.com/tswicegood/mysite-chp6.git
```

GitHub doesn't support HTTP, though, so if you try to clone it, you'll get an error from Git.

Choosing Networking Options

With the git protocol, SSH, and HTTP/HTTPS, it may seem like there are a lot of choices to determine which networking option you should use. Choosing one is straightforward, though:

- If you want speed above all else, you want the git protocol.
- If you value security above all else, SSH is the protocol for you.
- If you don't want to have to reconfigure restrictive firewalls, HTTP or HTTPS is the way to go.

Authentication is an issue. The git protocol is anonymous, so allowing a repository to be written using it means anyone can write to your repository. SSH requires proper user permissions for your repository to work, and HTTP/HTTPS requires a working WebDAV server.

You're not locked into one protocol, though. You can mix and match protocols to get an optimal balance of speed and security.

For my personal Git repository, I use a mixture of SSH and git. To write to my server, I use SSH keys for authenticating users and allow anonymous reads via the git protocol. Though the configuration may sound complex, it's made simple by a program called Gitosis, which we'll cover in Chapter 11, *Running a Git Server with Gitosis*, on page 143.

7.2 Cloning a Remote Repository

Sharing your work with other developers means you need a remote repository. The easiest way to work with a remote repository is to clone an existing repository. Cloning creates a local copy of the remote repository.

For projects that are already in progress, this is the normal route, but it isn't the only one. A remote repository can be configured later if you start working on a project by yourself and then need to share it. See the sidebar on page 98 for details.

Your local copy created by cloning works like it would if you had created it yourself using git init; the only difference is that you get the history of the repository up to the point you created the clone.

You use the git clone command any time you want to clone a repository to work with. In its simplest form, it takes only one parameter: the name of the repository you're cloning.

I'm sure you're familiar with this by now—there's been a git clone at the beginning of each chapter in Part II of this book. Let's clone one more time and grab the repository that we had from the previous chapter:

```
prompt> git clone git://github.com/tswicegood/mysite-chp6.git
Initialized empty Git repository in /work/mysite-chp6/.git/
remote: Counting objects: 37, done.
remote: Compressing objects: 100% (31/31), done.
remote: Total 37 (delta 10), reused 0 (delta 0)
Receiving objects: 100% (37/37), 4.08 KiB, done.
Resolving deltas: 100% (10/10), done.
```

This downloads the repository stored on the server and sets up a local copy of it in the mysite-chp6 directory. You can change into that directory and see the contents, the five files we created earlier:

```
prompt> cd mysite-chp6
prompt> ls
about.html   contact.html copy.txt     hello.html   original.txt
```

You now have a fully functioning clone of the remote repository that is set up to track both your own local changes and those you fetch from the remote server.

7.3 Keeping Up-to-Date

Cloning gets you the history of a repository up to the point you clone it, but other developers will still be making changes and updating the repository with those changes after you clone it.

You need to *fetch* those changes from the remote repository. You do this by using the git fetch command.

Fetching changes updates your remote branches. You can see your local branches when you run git branch. If you add the -r parameter, Git shows you the remote branches:

```
prompt> git branch -r
  origin/HEAD
  origin/master
```

You can check out those branches like a normal branch, but you should not change them. If you want to make a change to them, create a local branch from them first, and then make your change.

Running git fetch updates your remote branches; it doesn't merge the changes into your local branch. You can use git pull if you want to fetch the changes from a remote repository and merge them into your local branch at the same time.

git pull takes two parameters, the remote repository you want to pull from and the branch you want to pull—without the origin/ prefix.

Speaking of the origin/ prefix in the remote branch name, that's to keep the remote branches separate from your local branches. origin is the default remote repository name assigned to a repository that you create a clone from.

Now that you can fetch and pull changes from remote repositories, let's talk about pushing changes to a remote repository.

7.4 Pushing Changes

Getting changes from upstream repositories is only half of keeping in sync with everyone else on your team. You also need to be able to push changes back to an upstream repository to share the changes with everyone else.

As we talked about in Section 1.4, *Manipulating Files and Staying in Sync*, on page 6, pushing changes is sending changes to another repository. This is the step you go through to send your commits with another repository. It's an extra step from the traditional VCS world where a commit is automatically sent to a centralized repository.

Git makes a few assumptions when you call git push without any parameters. First, it assumes you're pushing to your origin repository. Second, it assumes you're pushing the current branch on your repository to its counterpart on the remote repository[1] if that branch exists remotely.

Git pushes only what has been checked in, so any changes you have in your working tree or have staged are not pushed:

```
prompt> git push
Counting objects: 11, done.
Compressing objects: 100% (7/7), done.
Writing objects: 100% (9/9), 933 bytes, done.
Total 9 (delta 0), reused 0 (delta 0)
Unpacking objects: 100% (9/9), done.
To /repos/mysite/.git
   5ef8232..d49d1e5  master -> master
```

You can add --dry-run to this command when you want to see what changes would be pushed.

You can also specify the repository you want to push to, just like git pull. The syntax is the same: git push <repository> <refspec>. The <repository> can be any valid repository. Any of the URLs we discussed (Section 7.1, *Network Protocols*, on page 91) will work, as will any named repository that we'll talk about in Section 7.5, *Adding New Remote Repositories*, on the facing page.

---

1. That's the default behavior; you can configure a branch to push to another one, but I'm going to let you work that one out on your own since it's not a normal case.

Retrieving Pushed Changes

It's not common, but there might be a case where you need to let someone push changes into your private repository. Or maybe you have to do it. I push changes between my private repositories in other virtual machines whenever I'm testing code in multiple OSs.

If changes are pushed into your repository—either by yourself or by someone else—those changes won't be reflected in your working tree. This keeps someone else from overwriting changes you have in your working tree that have not been committed yet.

You have to run git checkout HEAD to pull all the latest changes from the repository to your working tree. This gives you an opportunity to handle any conflicts through the methods we discussed in Section 5.4, *Handling Conflicts*, on page 64.

The <refspec> in its simplest form is a tag, a branch, or a special keyword such as HEAD. You can use it to specify which branches to push and where you want them to be pushed. For example, you can use git push origin mybranch:master to push the changes from mybranch to the remote master.

Now that you have the basics of cloning a repository and keeping your local repository in sync with remote repositories, let's cover one final topic, adding new repositories.

7.5 Adding New Remote Repositories

You can push or pull from any remote repository that you have read or write permission on. Typing the full name of a repository can be cumbersome, especially when you're syncing with the same repositories over and over again.

Your default remote repository is called origin. It's an alias to the full name of your repository—whatever you cloned. Say your team includes a developer named Erin, and you constantly pull changes from her repository.

Adding a Remote Repository Later

Starting to work on a project by cloning is great if the project already has a history, but how do you push your changes to a remote repository if you created it with git init?

Just add the repository you want to push to by using the git remote add command we covered in Section 7.5, *Adding New Remote Repositories*, on the preceding page. Call the remote repository origin if it is going to be the repository you want to push changes to by default.

For example, your session should look something like the following if you want to add a remote repository at git@example.com:/repos/pocus.git:

```
prompt> git remote add origin git@example.com:/repos/pocus.git
prompt> git push origin master
... output from Git ...
```

To do a one-off pull from her repository, you use git pull and her repository. It might look something like this:

```
prompt> git pull git://ourcompany.com/dev-erin.git
```

That's OK for a one-time pull, but if you're going to be doing it more than once, adding an alias can save some keystrokes. To add a new named remote repository, use git remote add <name> <repo-url>. This command adds Erin's repository:

```
prompt> git remote add erin git://ourcompany.com/dev-erin.git
```

Now, you can use erin instead of the full repository any time you need to push or pull some changes. So, the pull we just executed now looks like:

```
prompt> git pull erin HEAD
warning: no common commits
remote: Counting objects: 6318, done.
remote: Compressing objects: 100% (2114/2114), done.
remote: Total 6318 (delta 3899), reused 5680 (delta 3505)
Receiving objects: 100% (6318/6318), 1.03 MiB, done.
Resolving deltas: 100% (3899/3899), done.
From git://ourcompany.com/dev-erin.git
 * branch            HEAD       -> FETCH_HEAD
Merge made by recursive.
... a bunch of output showing the result of the pull ...
```

That's a lot easier to remember! Of course, erin is completely arbitrary. You can name it whatever you would like. The only limitation is that each name must be unique. You can have only one erin or origin.

You can use git remote add to add an origin to your repository if you don't have one. This is useful when you start a repository locally with git init and then need to send it to a remote repository later.

There are some other useful ways to use the git remote command too. You can call it without any parameters to see a list of all the remote aliases you have created, and git remote show <name> will show you some information on the remote repositories.

You can call git remote rm to remove a remote alias if you no longer need it or want to use that name for another repository.

That wraps up remote repositories and almost finishes up our tour of commands you need to know when using Git.

Chapter 8

Organizing Your Repository

Having the entire history of your project available to you is the key benefit to any version control system. You can quickly find old versions of the software and look through the history of a file to figure out how it got to its current state.

All this information can be overwhelming, though. A good strategy for organizing your repository is important to making sure you can find your way around all the history you create. This chapter explains how to do the following:

- Mark milestones within your project with tags
- Handle release branches to focus development when you're about to make a release
- Group your tags and branches in directory-like structures
- Track multiple projects using one or multiple repositories
- Use Git's submodules feature to track external repositories

This chapter uses the repository you've been working with. If you don't have the repository, you can clone the latest from GitHub:

```
prompt> git clone git://github.com/tswicegood/mysite-chp7.git
Initialized empty Git repository in /work/mysite-chp7/.git/
remote: Counting objects: 53, done.
remote: Compressing objects: 100% (47/47), done.
remote: Total 53 (delta 19), reused 0 (delta 0)
Receiving objects: 100% (53/53), 5.72 KiB, done.
Resolving deltas: 100% (19/19), done.
```

8.1 Marking Milestones with Tags

As your repository progresses, it is going to have milestones: it will be deployed, new versions will be created, and so on. Tags give you a convenient way to mark such milestones so you can come back to them later.

Tags act like bookmarks in your repository. You can use them to jump back to the point in the repository that you tagged. You can tag any commit in Git for any purpose you can think of.

The most common use of tags is to mark when the code in your project is released. That allows you to go back to the code you released if you need to fix or change something later.

Tags in Git are read-only, unlike the tags you might be familiar with if you're coming from Subversion. This means you can't make a change to the contents of a tag as if it were a normal branch. This is a much better way to handle tags. You can be sure that the tag is exactly what was tagged and hasn't changed since it was created.

The command to work with tags in Git is git tag. Just like git branch, you can call it without any parameters to see what tags you currently have:

```
prompt> git tag
1.0
```

That's the tag we created in Chapter 3, *Creating Your First Project*, on page 25. Let's create a tag called 1.1. To do that, call git tag again, but this time provide it with the tag name: 1.1:

```
prompt> git tag 1.1
```

Git does not provide any visible feedback that the tag was successfully created. You can call git tag without any parameters, though, to see your newly created tag:

```
prompt> git tag
1.0
1.1
```

Git's tag command may be quiet if it succeeds, but if there is a problem, it lets you know. For example, if you try to create a tag using a name that is not valid—a tag name with spaces, for example—it will display a fatal error such as this. Valid naming is discussed in Section 8.3, *Using Valid Names for Tags and Branches*, on page 106.

```
prompt> git tag "version 1.1"
fatal: 'version 1.1' is not a valid tag name.
```

Git creates a tag based on the current working tree's commit if you call it and provide only a tag name. You can provide it with an additional parameter to specify the commit you want to tag. The extra parameter can be any valid commit or branch name.

For example, you can create a tag from the latest commit in your contacts branch by calling git tag like this:

```
prompt> git tag contacts/1.1 contacts
prompt> git tag
1.0
1.1
contacts/1.1
```

You can use tags to return to the state of the repository that they marked. Even though you can't make changes to a tag, you can check it out like you would a branch:

```
prompt> git checkout 1.0
Note: moving to "1.0" which isn't a local branch
If you want to create a new branch from this checkout, you may do so
(now or later) by using -b with the checkout command again. Example:
  git checkout -b <new_branch_name>
HEAD is now at 4b53779... Add in a description element to the metadata
```

At this point, you're in a "no man's land" of sorts. You're not on a branch, so you can't track changes. If you run git branch to see your local branches, it will show that you are not on a branch:

```
prompt> git branch
* (no branch)
  about
  alternate
  contacts
  master
  new
```

You can create a new branch and check it out with git checkout -b like this:

```
prompt> git checkout -b from-1.0
Switched to a new branch "from-1.0"
```

Now you can start tracking changes directly again. Like all good things in Git, you can do this another way as well. You can create a new branch using git branch or git checkout -b and use a tag name as the second parameter:

```
prompt> git checkout -b another-from-1.0 1.0
Switched to a new branch "another-from-1.0"
```

The git log output here shows that the only commits in the current branch are the original three commits that were there for the 1.0 tag.

Creating a branch from a tag can be useful for creating *release branches* to fix bugs or make small changes to previously released code. Handling those release branches is the topic of the next section.

8.2 Handling Release Branches

Release branches are a place to prepare code for a release. Teams normally use them to segregate code for a release. What *segregate* means depends on the team.

The exact timing of a release branch depends on the team and your development style. For simplicity's sake, let's work with this definition: a release branch is created when a project is feature complete—that is, it has everything it needs to satisfy this release—but hasn't been fully vetted yet.

This type of branch will have only minimal changes made to it, and all will focus around fixes, whether they are bugs or logic, but no new features are added. These release branches make it easy to continue developing new features on the master branch while the team has a copy of the code that is about to be released without the new code in it.

Release branches are normally prefixed with an RB_ and contain the number of the release. So, a version 1.2 release would be RB_1.2, while the 1.3 version would be RB_1.3.

The release branch should last only for a short period while your release goes through any final testing. Once the release is ready, you create a tag to mark the occasion and delete the branch.

Don't worry about deleting the branch; you don't have to keep a branch around to keep that history. Your tag marks its place. There's no need to keep a branch around cluttering up your branch list.

What about fixing the inevitable bug that pops up in a release? You create a new release branch based on the tag like we did in the previous section. Use the RB_ prefix, and specify the tag you want to create it from.

```
prompt> git branch RB_1.0.1 1.0
prompt> git checkout RB_1.0.1
Switched to branch "RB_1.0.1"
```

All you did was use a tag name as the second parameter for git branch. It created a branch based on the commit the tag referenced.

Your new branch looks just like the release branch did when you created the tag. It has the same history as your release branch did before you deleted it.

You can check git log to show it:

```
prompt> git log --pretty=format:"%h %s"
4b53779 Add in a description element to the metadata
a5dacab add <head> and <title> to index
7b1558c add in hello world HTML
```

Now make your fix. Once you have the fix in place, create a new tag:

```
prompt> git tag 1.0.1
```

Once the bug is fixed and a new tag is created, you can delete the branch like you did with the previous release branch. You can't delete the branch you are on, so make sure to switch back to your master branch:

```
prompt> git checkout master
Switched to branch "master"
prompt> git branch -D RB_1.0.1
Deleted branch RB_1.0.1.
```

You might have noticed that git branch -D was used to delete the release branch. That's because master doesn't think it is related to RB_1.0.1 because of the new commit. We're going to leave it the way it is for a little bit longer—we'll fix it in Section 9.3, *Rebasing a Branch*, on page 118.

Release branches help organize your team's workflow as you approach a release. They allow you to insulate a release from any new features or bugs by making sure that only code that's necessary—bug fixes, final tweaks from client feedback, and so on—make it into the release before it happens.

And that's the mechanics of release branches in Git. The hard part is figuring out when to create the release branch. It depends on your organization's development style. If you're constantly adding new features, creating a branch as soon as the product is "feature complete" might be a good idea; however, if your development process is a little bit slower, you might be able to wait to create the release branch until a few days before the release.

Getting the timing just right is an art. Git's easy merging that we talked about in Section 5.3, *Merging Changes Between Branches*, on page 59 means that if you branch too early, keeping the two branches in sync will be a snap, and if you realize you should have branched earlier, create the branch from the commit where you should have branched at.

Release branches and tags can help you organize your repository. The only thing you have to watch out for is how to name them. Git is pretty permissive in what it allows, but there are a few gotchas. We'll cover those next.

8.3 Using Valid Names for Tags and Branches

Let's talk about valid names for tags and branches before we jump off into some specific types of organization you can employ in Git. Git is pretty liberal in what you can do, but there are a few things to avoid.

First, you can use a forward slash (/) in a tag or branch name, but it can't end with the slash. This allows you to organize tags and branches into directory-like structures.

You can also use periods (.) in the name, but Git will not allow the first portion of a path element in the name to begin with a period. This means that releases/1.0 is a valid tag name, but neither releases/.1.0 nor .releases/1.0 is.

If you're familiar with the file system on Linux or BSD/Mac OS X, you probably recognize the issue with the second name. Those operating systems treat a file or directory that begins with a period as something that should be hidden.

You can't use some special characters in a tag or branch name. These include spaces, tildes (~), carets (^), colons (:), question marks (?), asterisks (*), and opening brackets ([). None of the ASCII control characters (anything lower than \040) or the Delete key (ASCII \177) is allowed. Don't worry if you don't know what those are, or how to create them, because it means you'll probably never create them by accident!

The only other rule in naming is that you can't use a double period anywhere in the name. Remember the syntax for ranges we talked about in Section 6.2, *Specifying Revision Ranges*, on page 73? Ranges use the <first-commit>..<second-commit> syntax. These aren't allowed in tag and branch names to keep from having any ambiguity.

That's it. Branches and tags can be named about anything that is a valid file or directory name, just like your normal file system, and you can organize them into directory-like structures to help sort them. Of course, we haven't gotten into the specifics of tags yet, so let's cover them.

8.4 Tracking Multiple Projects

Most organizations have multiple projects. Even if they are different parts of one product, they all need to be segregated so everyone on the team can find the code they need without having to sift through all the code.

You can handle multiple projects with Git in a couple of ways. You can store all your projects in one repository, or you can have individual repositories for each project. There are pros and cons to each, and we'll cover them in the following sections.

Multiple Projects, One Repository

The first and most straightforward method is creating one repository and storing multiple projects within it. You can do this by creating a different top-level directory for each project within your repository.

This will be familiar to those with a Subversion background because this is how Subversion handles multiple projects within a repository. This is a convenient way to store all the projects together so you have to clone only one repository to get access to everything.

This works well for projects that need to have a common history, such as a project that is made up of several components that are all released together.

It could be a CMS, an order entry system, or any other type of program that consists of several distinct components that are all released at one time as a package.

Notice that I keep talking about releasing at the same time. This is the criteria I use for determining whether a repository should contain one or multiple projects like we'll discuss in Section 8.4, *Multiple Projects, Multiple Repositories*, on the following page.

If each smaller project, or component, is only ever released as part of the larger project, then sharing the same history might be a good idea.

This makes sure that all the history in the repository revolves around one project.

If they are released separately, then they probably need their own history. The distinction is made because of the way tags and branches are handled within Git. They refer to the whole repository, not one section of it.

With multiple projects on independent release schedules, the number of branches and tags you have to create will increase exponentially. Repositories are lightweight in Git, though, so creating one repository for each project isn't difficult.

Multiple Projects, Multiple Repositories

Creating one repository per project is the alternative to trying to store multiple projects with one repository. This requires a little more setup but allows each project to have its own independent history.

Determining when to split a project is a straightforward process. Flip the rule on keeping all projects in one repository. Will this project be released by itself? If it will, it needs to be in its own repository.

This isn't a rule set in stone. If you release the two projects independently but they are so coupled that you can't use one without the other, sometimes it is more convenient to have them in one repository so you have to clone only the one.

Like everything in Git, there is yet another way to handle this situation. That brings us to our next topic: Git submodules.

8.5 Using Git Submodules to Track External Repositories

Sometimes you need to track multiple repositories as if they're all in the same repository. This might be because of a dependency on some third-party library or possibly because your in-house project has been divided into multiple projects to help make them more manageable.

Git allows you to track external repositories through what it calls *submodules*. These allow you to store a repository within another repository while keeping the two histories completely independent. Those coming from a Subversion background might recognize these as `svn:externals`.

Adding a New Submodule

Let's demonstrate this behavior. First we need to create a new repository that will house our submodule repository. Let's create a repository called magic:

```
prompt> mkdir /work/magic
prompt> cd /work/magic
prompt> git init
Initialized empty Git repository in /work/magic/.git/
```

With this empty repository initialized, you can use git submodule to view the submodules associated with this repository:

```
prompt> git submodule
prompt>
```

Since there are no submodules defined yet, it doesn't return anything. Adding a new submodule is straightforward. You use the git submodule add command. It has two required parameters. The first is the repository; the second is the path where you want to store the repository.

For example, let's add the hocus repository—a small repository hosted on GitHub that I created to use for the book. And to keep things clear, let's put it in the hocus directory. You can use the command on one line without the \; those are here to make the command fit on the page:

```
prompt> git submodule add \
        git://github.com/tswicegood/hocus.git \
        hocus
Initialized empty Git repository in /work/magic/hocus/.git/
remote: Counting objects: 7, done.
remote: Compressing objects: 100% (5/5), done.
remote: Total 7 (delta 0), reused 7 (delta 0)
Receiving objects: 100% (7/7), done.
```

Now when you rerun git submodule, hocus is displayed:

```
prompt> git submodule
-20cc9ddc65b5f3ea3b871480c1e6d8085db48457 hocus
```

Git submodules track a particular revision within the remote repository. That revision is noted here by the hash, and then the name you gave it (hocus) is displayed. You probably noticed the minus sign before the hash. This is telling you that the hocus submodule has not been initialized. That's simple enough to fix:

```
prompt> git submodule init hocus
Submodule 'hocus' (git://github.com/tswicegood/hocus.git)
registered for path 'hocus'
```

This adds an entry to .git/config so Git understands that the hocus directory contains a submodule. Now with everything added and initialized, you can see that you have some changes in your repository:

```
prompt> git status
# On branch master
#
# Initial commit
#
# Changes to be committed:
#   (use "git rm --cached <file>..." to unstage)
#
#       new file: .gitmodules
#       new file: hocus
#
```

The .gitmodules is a plain-text file that stores all the information about your submodule. Git tracks this file inside the repository. That way, when you share your repository with someone else, Git has the information it needs to get their submodule set up too.

Now it's time to commit these changes. Any simple log message will do:

```
prompt> git commit -m "initial commit with submodule"
Created initial commit f24a0d9: initial commit with submodule
 2 files changed, 4 insertions(+), 0 deletions(-)
 create mode 100644 .gitmodules
 create mode 160000 hocus
```

Now your submodule is ready to share with other repositories. Creating a clone of a repository with submodules is a little different, so let's try it.

Cloning a Repository with Submodules

A few extra steps are required to set up submodules on a freshly cloned repository. Let's walk through it here. First things first—create a clone of the magic repository:

```
prompt> cd /work
prompt> git clone magic new-magic
Initialized empty Git repository in /work/new-magic/.git/
prompt> cd new-magic
prompt> ls
hocus
```

You can see that the hocus directory is there, but it's empty if you look in it. Running git submodule shows that it hasn't been initialized:

```
prompt> git submodule
-20cc9ddc65b5f3ea3b871480c1e6d8085db48457 hocus
```

Remember from the previous section that the minus sign as the first character shows that a submodule hasn't been initialized. Run the git submodule init command to initialize it:

```
prompt> git submodule init hocus
Submodule 'hocus' (git://github.com/tswicegood/hocus.git)
registered for path 'hocus'
```

The hocus directory is still empty, though. There's one more command required to pull the changes into your submodule: git submodule update. Just like the other git submodule commands, this takes the name of the submodule you're working with as its parameter.

```
prompt> git submodule update hocus
Initialized empty Git repository in /work/new-magic/hocus/.git/
remote: Counting objects: 7, done.
remote: Compressing objects: 100% (5/5), done.
remote: Total 7 (delta 0), reused 7 (delta 0)
Receiving objects: 100% (7/7), done.
Submodule path 'hocus': checked out
'20cc9ddc65b5f3ea3b871480c1e6d8085db48457'
```

Now your hocus directory has all the files from the 20cc9dd commit that you tracked. This brings you up to speed on how to set up a submodule, but right now it always tracks this one commit. What do you do when you want to change what you want to use? That's up next.

Changing Which Commit Is Tracked by a Submodule

Git's submodules don't track the latest commit in the repository; they track an individual commit. It always starts tracking whatever the HEAD —the latest commit—is when you add the submodule. You have to tell Git when you want to change the commit it's tracking.

This might seem odd at first for those with a Subversion background. Subversion tracks the repository and automatically pulls the latest commit whenever you run an update. To track an individual revision, you have to explicitly set that up.

That might seem more convenient at first glance, but it can introduce problems. What happens when a bug is introduced in the repository you were tracking or when you have one revision of a remote repository and another developer has a different version? Explicitly tracking one commit removes those issues.

Git determines the commit when you create the submodule; then it *detaches* from the repository. A submodule is actually a completely cloned repository that is checked out at one particular commit. You can see this by changing into the hocus directory and looking at the branch list:

```
prompt> cd hocus/
prompt> git branch
* (no branch)
  master
```

This repository has only two commits in it, so let's change to the first commit instead of the second. Just check out the commit before HEAD:

```
prompt> git checkout HEAD^
Previous HEAD position was 20cc9dd... initial commit
HEAD is now at 7901f67... initial commit with README
```

Now you have to tell Git that this is the changed version you want to use. You can see that Git realizes there's a change by running git submodule without any parameters:

```
prompt> cd ..
prompt> git submodule
+7901f67feaadeeef755734a92febbc7214fb7871 hocus (7901f67)
```

The + is the note that this commit isn't the one that Git expects. git status also shows that the hocus directory has changed:

```
prompt> git status
# On branch master
# Changed but not updated:
#   (use "git add <file>..." to update what will be committed)
#
#       modified:   hocus
#
no changes added to commit (use "git add" and/or "git commit -a")
```

All you have to do now is add the hocus directory and commit the change. That tells Git you want to track the submodule using the new commit.

```
prompt> git add hocus
prompt> git commit -m 'update commit to track in submodule'
Created commit fedf2bc: update commit to track in submodule
 1 files changed, 1 insertions(+), 1 deletions(-)
```

Check out the patch for that commit. You'll see the changes that Git recorded. Pay special attention when updating the commit that a submodule should track. There are a few things to keep in mind when working with submodules.

Gotchas to Watch Out For with Submodules

Make sure you don't include a trailing slash with calling git add. Git currently translates that into a request to add all the files from that repository into your current local repository instead of updating the commit a submodule should track. A quick check of git status prior to a commit will show when this mistake has been made.

Another thing to keep in mind is that git submodule update is destructive. Running the update command will overwrite any changes you have in your submodule that have not been committed. Be sure to double-check your submodule's working tree for changes before running git submodule update to correct changes.

The other gotchas revolve around adding new content directly to a submodule's repository. First, before you make a change, check out the branch you want to apply the changes to. Remember that the submodule is detached from the normal branches. A quick git checkout will fix that.

Then, once your changes have been committed, you have to make sure your changes are available from the remote repository before you share your changes to the submodule checkout. Git will behave unexpectedly if the commit of your submodule references is not available from the remote repository when you try to run git submodule update.

That brings us to the end of this chapter on organization. You learned how to use tags for the first time and how you can use them to organize the milestones of your repository. You also learned about release branches and how they can help you organize your repository as you prepare for a release.

Now you know that there are two different ways to organize your repositories and projects: storing everything in one big repository and storing everything in individual repositories. The chapter closed with a look at Git submodules and how you can use them to track remote repositories as independent parts of your repository.

With what you learned in this and the previous chapters, you now know what you need to about Git to start being productive with it. In the next chapter, we'll cover a few of the lesser-used parts of Git that you need to know to round out your knowledge.

Chapter 9

Beyond the Basics

Git is a rich toolkit. So far in this book we've covered how to use the day-to-day features of Git—the basics. That barely scratches the surface of Git.

Git currently ships with more than 140 different commands. Many you will probably never have to use. Commands such as git check-ref-format, which Git uses internally to determine whether a string is a valid branch or tag name, is of use only to those creating extensions to Git.

But there are some commands that you won't use every day that are extremely useful when you do need them. This chapter is devoted to those topics, which include the following:

- Compacting your repository history
- Exporting your repository
- Rebasing a branch's history against its parent
- Using the reflog to fix your repository
- Bisecting your repository to find what change introduced a bug

This chapter uses the mysite repository you've been creating throughout the book. If you haven't been following along, you can create a clone of the work that's been done up to this point by using the following command:

```
prompt> git clone git://github.com/tswicegood/mysite-chp8.git
Initialized empty Git repository in /work/mysite-chp8/.git/
remote: Counting objects: 56, done.
remote: Compressing objects: 100% (49/49), done.
remote: Total 56 (delta 21), reused 0 (delta 0)
Receiving objects: 100% (56/56), 5.92 KiB, done.
Resolving deltas: 100% (21/21), done.
```

9.1 Compacting Repository History

Everything in life needs a little maintenance to work optimally. Your car needs its oil changed, your floors need sweeping, and Git needs to have git gc run.

Git stores *everything*. The problem with this is that it occasionally will have some leftover data that is no longer useful. For example, when you use the --amend parameter on git commit to fix a commit, Git remembers the older revision too. Or you delete an experimental branch using the git branch -D, and Git knows what was in that branch even though nothing references it any longer.

This is where git gc comes in. Once a month, or about every 100 or so commits, it's a good idea to run git gc to tidy things up by optimizing the way Git stores its history internally. It doesn't change the history, only the way it is stored.

Running git gc with an empty repository won't hurt anything, but it won't accomplish much either. To give our examples some meat, I'm going to use the repository my book is stored in.

I hadn't run git gc on my book's repository for a few weeks when I started writing this section. In those few weeks, I had made quite a few additions along with 50 or so small commits fixing errata that had been reported by my great beta book readers. Here's what the git gc output on my book's repository looks like:

```
prompt> git gc
Counting objects: 3918, done.
Compressing objects: 100% (2052/2052), done.
Writing objects: 100% (3918/3918), done.
Total 3918 (delta 2103), reused 3440 (delta 1852)
Removing duplicate objects: 100% (256/256), done.
```

Your output will vary slightly, of course, based on the size of your repository's history. The changes that git gc makes stick with your repository. Once it has been run, you don't need to run it again until there are more changes that need to be optimized.

So, what does this optimization translate into? Disk space. Running the git gc command on my book's repository reduced the size of the repository by roughly 20 percent!

This isn't to say that Git normally isn't efficient. The problem is that Git wants to be fast and efficient. To achieve both, it delegates some of the optimizations to later so you can run them when speed isn't an issue.

You can add the --aggressive parameter to git gc to do even further optimizations. This comes at the expense of speed but can be worth it.

Git stores changes that were made in what it calls *deltas*. git gc compresses those deltas when it runs by itself, but it doesn't recalculate them. Adding --aggressive tells Git to recalculate those deltas from scratch when it runs its optimization.

9.2 Exporting Your Repository

On a successful project, you have to release the software you're creating. If the software is written in one of the modern scripting languages such as Python or Ruby or PHP, you have to include the source for the end user to be able to run it.

You can do this by providing access to your public Git repositories, but creating official "releases" that are snapshots of your project reduces the amount of knowledge needed for your user to get up and running with your software.

Git provides a convenient tool for creating such a snapshot—git archive. It exports your code in either tar or zip format, creating an exact copy of your repository at the point you give it.

git archive takes a few parameters. First, you have to specify the format you want by specifying the --format=<format-type> parameter. Valid format types are tar and zip.

Second, you must supply a point in the history of the repository you want to create the archive from. This can be a commit, a branch, or a tag. That's all you have to provide, but another useful parameter is --prefix. Using that, you can specify what you want the files that are exported to be prefixed with. You can use this to put your release in a particular directory.

For example, you can create an archive of the mysite repository you've been working on. Execute this command from within the working tree of your repository:

```
prompt> git archive --format=zip \
                    --prefix=mysite-release/ \
                    HEAD > mysite-release.zip
```

The first line contains the --format parameter we talked about. The second contains the --prefix parameter. Notice that there's a trailing forward slash at the end of mysite-release/. Without that, git archive adds the string to the beginning of every filename rather than putting it in a directory.

The last line has two parts. First, it specifies the commit you are creating the archive from—HEAD. After that, it tells your shell to put the output from git archive into the mysite-release.zip file by using >, which is a greater-than symbol.

The command to create a tarball, or tar, of your repository is similar. You have to provide an additional command instead of directing the output of git archive directly to the file. You can create a mysite-release.tar.gz file by executing this command:

```
prompt> git archive --format=tar \
                    --prefix=mysite-release/ \
                    HEAD | gzip > mysite-release.tar.gz
```

Notice that after HEAD, you use the pipe (|) to pass the contents to the gzip command, which then generates the mysite-release.tar.gz file. You can replace gzip with bzip2 to use bzip2 compression instead of gzip.

Exporting your repository as either a tarball or as a zip file gives you a convenient way to distribute a snapshot of your repository to people who don't need, or in some cases don't want, the entire history of your repository.

9.3 Rebasing a Branch

Branches are a great way to organize your work, but keeping everything in sync between branches has been branching's Achilles' heel. With merge tracking, such as Git provides, the effort required to keep everything in sync is greatly reduced, but there is another way.

For example, in Section 8.2, *Handling Release Branches*, on page 104, you added code to the RB_1.0.1 branch. There's a new paragraph that exists in the 1.0.1 tag that master doesn't know about yet.

You can rebase master against that tag so that the change is incorporated into the history of the master branch, as if the master had always had that change.

We talked about git rebase earlier in Section 6.7, *Rewriting History*, on page 85 where you used git rebase -i to interactively rewrite the history. You can use it without the -i parameter to tell Git to *rebase* (or rewrite) the history in your current branch against an updated point on another branch. Think of it as a way to replay the history of your branch as if it were created at the new updated point in your repository's history.

Let's start the rebase. Run git rebase, and provide it with the tag you're going to rebase against:

```
prompt> git rebase 1.0.1
First, rewinding head to replay your work on top of it...
Applying: add in a bio link
error: patch failed: index.html:5
error: index.html: patch does not apply
Using index info to reconstruct a base tree...
Falling back to patching base and 3-way merge...
Auto-merged index.html
CONFLICT (content): Merge conflict in index.html
Failed to merge in the changes.
Patch failed at 0001.

When you have resolved this problem run "git rebase --continue".
If you would prefer to skip this patch, instead run "git rebase --skip".
To restore the original branch and stop rebasing run "git rebase
--abort".
```

Oops. There's an error right off the bat. Remember, we covered handling conflicts in Section 5.4, *Handling Conflicts*, on page 64. Using the git mergetool is the normal course to take here, but editing by hand is going to be easier this time.

That's because there isn't a right or wrong change. You want both the new paragraph from 1.0.1 and the unordered list that you added after creating the 1.0 tag.

Editing the file by hand is the easiest way here. Your index.html file has this conflict in it:

```
<<<<<<< HEAD:index.html
    <p>
        Fixed
    </p>
=======
    <ul>
        <li><a href="bio.html">Biography</a></li>
    </ul>
>>>>>>> add in a bio link:index.html
```

Remove the three lines that signify the conflict so it reads like a normal file. After you save the file, run the following to tell Git the conflict is resolved and to continue rebasing:

```
prompt> git add index.html
```

```
prompt> git rebase --continue
Applying: add in a bio link
... a bunch of additional lines saying Applying: ...
Applying: copy original to show cross-file blame
```

Remember how you renamed index.html to hello.html using git mv in Section 4.4, *Managing Files*, on page 51? Check your hello.html file now. It now contains the new paragraph that was added in 1.0.1.

This is a pretty simple case. There was only the initial conflict, and then the changes were pretty straightforward. Let's look at a few of the more complex cases.

Say that you're following the Git repository of your favorite language or framework. You might be maintaining a branch with some custom changes on top of the normal code. There's a couple of things that might happen.

First, if you submitted one of your changes and it was accepted, Git is smart enough to realize that the change has been applied. It won't try to apply your change again if it's already been made.

Another possibility is a conflict. You dealt with a simple conflict; the process is always the same. Fix the conflict, and then call the git add and git rebase --continue like you did.

Of course, you can also call git rebase with --skip or --abort to either skip that particular commit or completely abandon the rebase process, respectively.

The --onto parameter provides another interesting way to rewrite your history. For example, you have three branches: master, the contacts branch that was created from master, and the search branch that was created from contacts.

The history of those branches might go something like this. You started with contact code, but partway into it you decide to add new search code too.

After you finish with the new search code, you realize that it would work directly without requiring any of the changes that are in your contact branch.

This is what the --onto parameter does. It takes one parameter, the branch you want to rebase onto. Your command to rebase search onto the master branch looks like this:

```
prompt> git rebase --onto master contact search
```

This breaks the search branch off the contact branch and moves it to the master branch. This is useful if you need to merge the search branch back into master but don't need everything in the contact branch. Of course, search has to be completely independent to keep from having any merge conflicts when the rebase starts replaying the changes.

You can do some other interesting things with --onto and a combination of commit ranges like we discussed in Section 6.2, *Specifying Revision Ranges*, on page 73. For example, you can erase a revision by using git rebase. To erase the commit two commits ago, you can do this:

```
prompt> git rebase --onto HEAD^^ HEAD^ HEAD
```

This rebases onto the commit that happened two commits prior to your current HEAD, starting one commit ago through the current HEAD.

Of course, any time you start rewriting the history of a branch, it's a good idea to have a backup plan in case things go wrong. You can create additional branches to experiment in before you do them in your live branches. Since branches are so cheap in Git, it's a good idea to use them instead of live branches when you experiment with rebasing.

There is another tool that comes in handy if things go wrong: the reflog.

9.4 Using the Reflog

One of the key tenets that Linus set for Git was that it had to be safe. Being nondestructive means you have to be able to get back to any state in the repository, and to do that, you need to have some mechanism for tracking the changes in state.

The normal history of a repository will protect you in all but the most extreme cases with a normal version control system. Git allows you to do things that most VCSs can't. Changing the order of commits, breaking one commit into multiple commits, removing commits, adding extra ones—these are all tasks that Git does that a VCS like Subversion or CVS can't.

Of course, with all this power comes some risk. What happens when you accidentally delete a branch using git branch -D or a git rebase -i goes wrong?[1] This is where Git's reflog comes in.

1. This happened to your humble author the first time he did an interactive rebase. About fifty commits disappeared in about five seconds and weren't retrieved until he got familiar with git reflog.

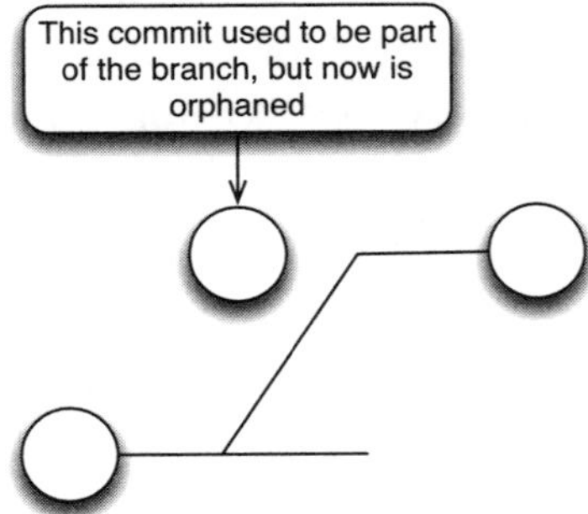

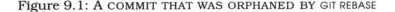

Figure 9.1: A COMMIT THAT WAS ORPHANED BY GIT REBASE

The reflog keeps track of when a branch changes. Remember in Chapter 5, *Understanding and Using Branches*, on page 55 that we talked about how branches are only a pointer to the latest commit in that line? The reflog tracks all those changes. Viewing it, you can find the commit you need to check out to restore a branch.

For example, let's create a simple repository and mess it up. Create a new repository with a single commit, and then create a branch and add two more commits. The contents can be whatever you want; you just need the commits in place.

Now, using git rebase or git rebase -i, which you read about in Section 9.3, *Rebasing a Branch*, on page 118 and Section 6.7, *Rewriting History*, on page 85, delete the first of your commits on the second branch. Now your branch should look like Figure 9.1.

You can verify what your repository's history looks like by using git log.

That history is what you expect. After git rebase -i deleted the one commit, there are two commits in the history. Now check the reflog; you'll see it knows about a lot more commits:

```
prompt> git reflog
1b41334... HEAD@{0}: commit: third commit
5e685de... HEAD@{1}: checkout: moving from reflog to 5e685de...
0cb04ad... HEAD@{2}: commit: third commit
71bc515... HEAD@{3}: commit: second commit
5e685de... HEAD@{4}: checkout: moving from master to reflog
```

I shortened the commit on the second line of the output so it would fit on the page. This output reads in reverse chronological order, like the regular git log. Notice that there are two commits with the message third commit. Commit 0cb04ad is the first commit, while 1b41334 is the second commit after git rebase removed 71bc515.

So, to restore to your first third commit, all you have to do is check out that commit:

```
prompt> git checkout 0cb04ad
Note: moving to "0cb04ad" which isn't a local branch
If you want to create a new branch from this checkout, you may do so
(now or later) by using -b with the checkout command again. Example:
  git checkout -b <new_branch_name>
HEAD is now at 0cb04ad... third commit
```

As the message tells you, you're not on a real branch, but you can create one here with a simple git checkout -b. Not being on a branch doesn't stop you from viewing the history, though. Using git log, you can now see your second commit has been restored.

```
prompt> git log --pretty=format:"%h %s"
0cb04ad third commit
71bc515 second commit
5e685de initial commit
```

Of course, you don't have to explicitly check out the branch to create it. You can just as easily use git branch to create the branch immediately if you don't need to check the history prior to creating the branch:

```
prompt> git branch reflog-restored 0cb04ad
prompt> git checkout reflog-restored
Switched to branch "reflog-restored"
```

git gc, which we talked about in Section 9.1, *Compacting Repository History*, on page 116, will cause some older reflog entries to expire. For example, the commits we just restored are normally deleted after thirty days. This can be changed by changing the gc.reflogExpireUnreachable config setting. Likewise, normal reflog entries are expired after ninety days, unless you change gc.reflogExpire to something else. That is to keep the reflog from getting too large.

You'll rarely need to use the reflog, but when you do, it can be a life-saver. Rewriting history can be dangerous, and git reflog is a safety net to help keep you safe from yourself.

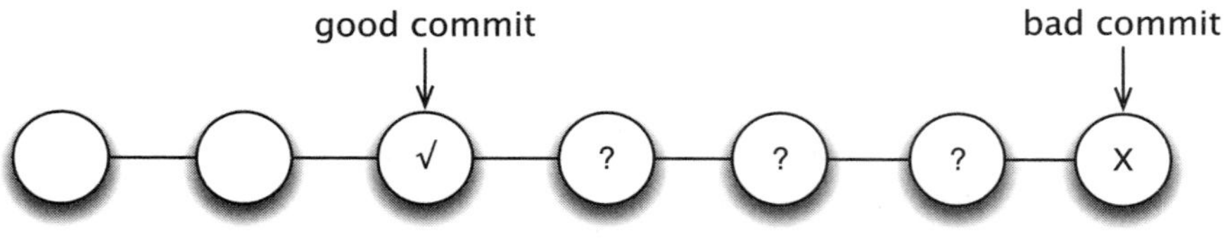

Figure 9.2: REPOSITORY WITH A KNOWN GOOD COMMIT AND A KNOWN BAD COMMIT

9.5 Bisecting Your Repository

Try as we might, bugs still make it into the software we create. We add unit tests, have rigorous acceptance tests created with clients, and think through the implications of what we are creating, but all of these steps require perfection from humans in order to work.

Plan for the occasional bug. All those tools can help you locate the bug, but when they fail, you can turn to your repository to try to figure out when the bug got introduced. `git bisect` is a tool that helps with that process.

`git bisect` works by stepping through your repository's history based on a known bad commit and a known good commit. It walks you through your repository, letting you mark a commit as good or bad, until you isolate the commit that created the bug.

Consider this example. Your repository for your project has a `1.0` tag, and your current code is working toward the 1.1 release of your project. Your beta testers reported a bug in the new releases that they can't reproduce in version 1.0 of your software. Now you have a good point and a bad point in your repository to check against, so you can use `git bisect` to start walking through the history to isolate the bug.

You can see what this repository looks like in Figure 9.2. You can see that there are three possible commits that caused this break.

First things first—create a test case that demonstrates the bug. Test it against the bad commit to make sure it doesn't pass, and then test it against the one you know is good to prove that it works there.

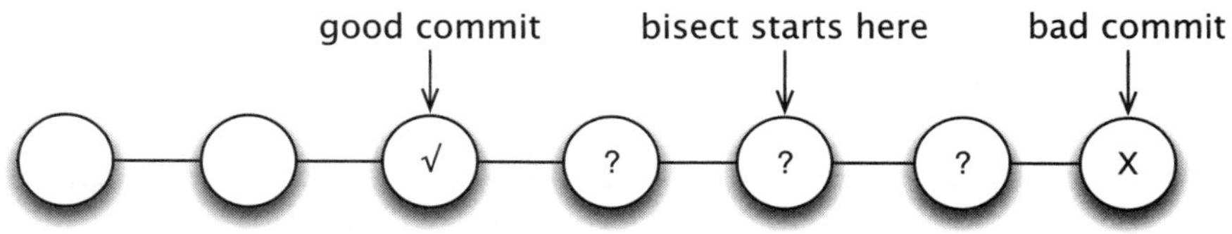

Figure 9.3: GIT BISECT STARTS IN THE MIDDLE.

Now, move back to the bad commit and start the bisect process by calling git bisect start, then git bisect bad, and finally git bisect good <some commit or tag>. The session looks something like this:

```
prompt> git bisect start
prompt> git bisect bad
prompt> git bisect good 1.0
Bisecting: 1 revisions left to test after this
[d3289f8ab4916f58134a7e5c813ca91c13dd6a70] <commit message>
```

Once you mark the second commit, git bisect moves you to another place in the repository. It takes the commits between the two known points, splits them in half, and checks out that point. This makes your repository look like Figure 9.3.

Now rerun your tests to prove this commit good or bad. In this case, the commit is bad, so mark it as such with git bisect bad:

```
prompt> git bisect bad
Bisecting: 0 revisions left to test after this
[1318fa48089ea36c082d7e69cbd7c04b489821ec] <commit message>
```

Now, there is just one commit left to try with no more commits left between this and the good commit. Logically, you can determine at this point that if the previous commit was good and all the commits after this point are bad, this one must be the cause. A quick run of the unit tests proves that it is.

Marking it as bad causes Git to realize it has hit the last possible bad commit and shows the log entry for it. Now you've narrowed the history down to the commit that was bad. All that's left to do is figure out exactly which change in the commit caused the problem and fix it.

git bisect moves you off your branch as it steps through each commit. You need to move back onto the branch before you apply your change.

You do that with git bisect reset:

```
prompt> git bisect reset
Switched to branch "master"
```

Of course, like all interesting things in Git, there's more to git bisect than just the simple case. When trying to understand the history of your changes, having a visualization of the history can be helpful. For this, you can use git bisect visualize.

You can use git bisect log to show the history of what commits have been marked as good or bad if text output is more your style. It also comes in handy if you find out later that you've made a mistake in marking a commit as either good or bad.

To do that, save the output of git bisect log to a file, and then remove all the output after the point of your mistake. Then supply that file as the parameter to git bisect replay <some-file> to tell Git to replay the history up to that point.

All of this is great, but a lot of manual work is involved. Not only does it add to the amount of work you have to do, but it also makes it more error prone because of human error. An automated test suite helps, but git bisect can take it a step further by automating the running of that test suite for you.

To do this, you need to have a script that can be run from the command line that exits with a 0 exit code when the tests pass or a positive number if the tests fail. The normal practice is to exit with a 1.

You can't exit with the exit code 125 unless you want to skip a commit and have git bisect move to the next commit. Generally, you do not want to skip a commit unless you just can't test whether a commit is good or bad.

git bisect run is the command you use to automatically run this script. For example, if you create a script called run-tests, you can invoke it like this:

```
prompt> git bisect start HEAD 1.0
Bisecting: 1 revisions left to test after this
[d3289f8ab4916f58134a7e5c813ca91c13dd6a70] <commit message>
prompt> git bisect run /work/run-tests
running /work/run-tests
```

git bisect continues running just like you were doing it manually, except it uses the exit value from the script called /work/run-tests. Every time the script returns an integer other than 0, it is treated as a bad commit.

Notice that this command references a file in another directory. This is to make sure Git doesn't change the file that git bisect run is trying to execute. Using a file outside the repository to drive your tests isn't a necessity but can help avoid any problems.

git bisect is one of those commands that you may never have to use, but if you do, it can be a lifesaver. Coupled with an automated test suite that can be run from the command line, you can use it to trace bugs quickly.

The enterprising development team could even tie it into their automated build system to help isolate bugs. This can be a tremendous time-saver when a project moves too rapidly to be tested with a traditional continuous integration system where each change kicks off a new build.

This brings us to the end of the basics chapter and the end of Part II. Whether you've just started your journey as a developer and are learning your first VCS or you are an old hand looking to pick up Git, you now know what you need to start being productive with Git.

Part III covers administrative tasks. It's required reading only if you plan on migrating to Git from Subversion or CVS—covered in Chapter 10, *Migrating to Git*, on page 131—or are going to set up your own remote repository—covered in Chapter 11, *Running a Git Server with Gitosis*, on page 143.

Part III

Administration

Chapter 10

Migrating to Git

If you've been developing for long, you probably have a Subversion or CVS repository that already has your complete project history stored in it. Switching to Git doesn't mean you have to lose all that history. In fact, Git provides several tools to make migrating easy.

In this chapter, you'll learn how to do the following:

- Import your history from Subversion
- Stay in sync with a remote Subversion
- Import your history from CVS

To help you map the Subversion and CVS commands you're familiar with to their Git counterparts, the Subversion mapping is shown in Figure 10.1, on the next page, and the CVS mapping is shown in Figure 10.2, on page 133.

10.1 Communicating with SVN

Many companies today use Subversion to manage their version control repositories. It was designed to be a compelling replacement to CVS and has succeeded in many areas. It is much easier to understand with its clear, understandable command structure, and its atomic commits are much easier to track.

Git didn't set out to become a replacement to Subversion—or any other version control system, for that matter—but its features make it a "compelling replacement" to Subversion.

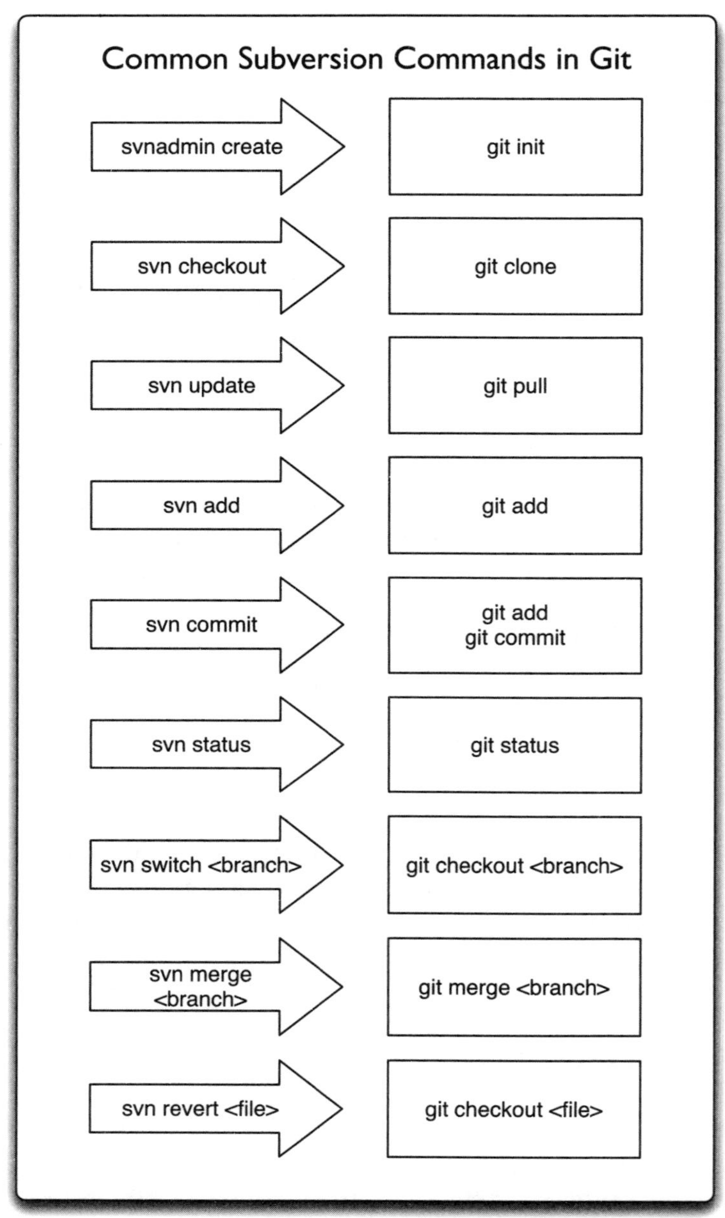

Figure 10.1: COMMON SUBVERSION COMMANDS IN GIT

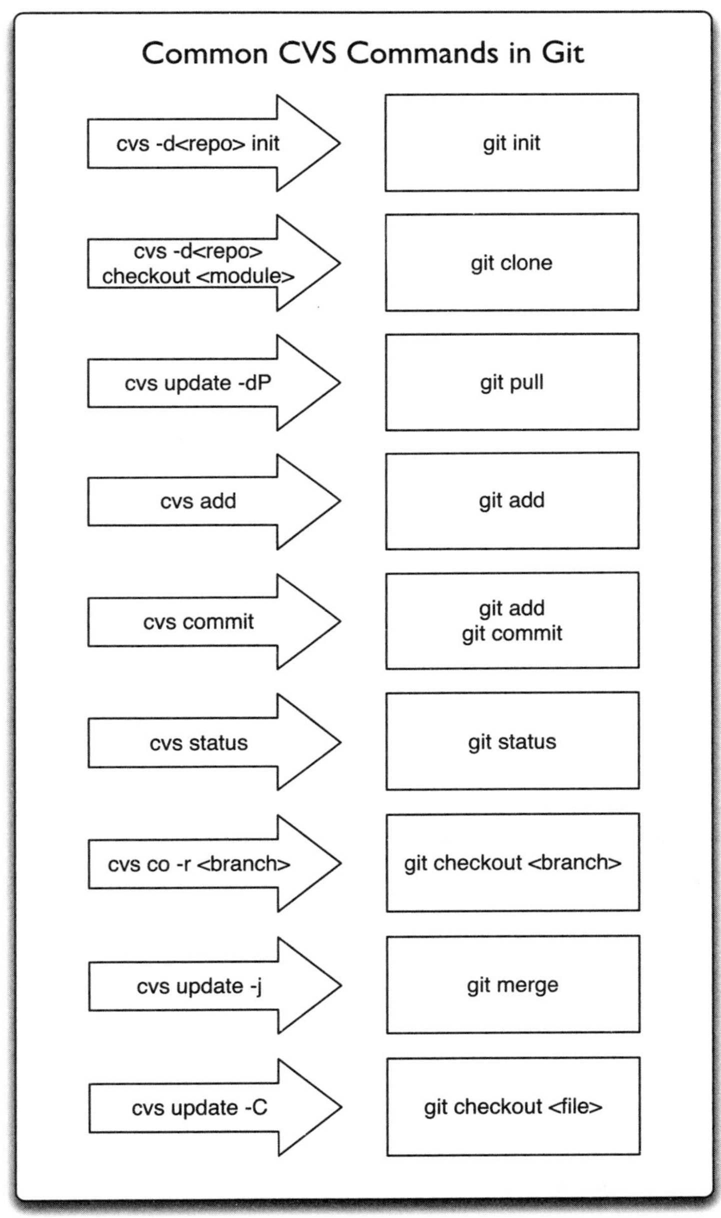

Figure 10.2: COMMON CVS COMMANDS IN GIT

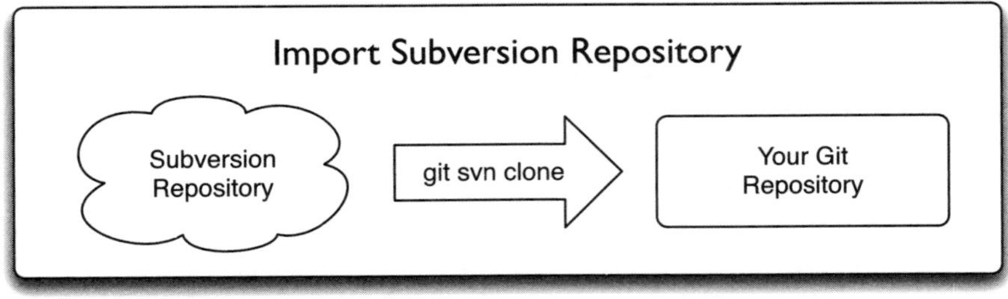

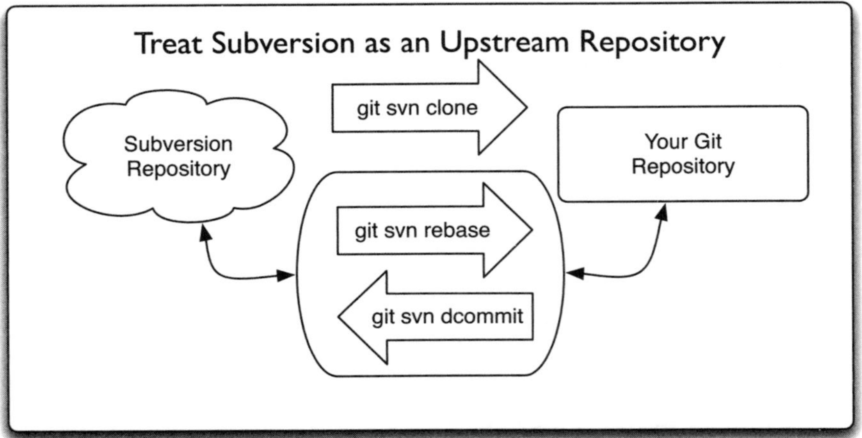

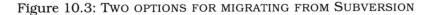

Figure 10.3: TWO OPTIONS FOR MIGRATING FROM SUBVERSION

A quick note before we start: when reading this chapter, you'll see references to both git-svn and `git svn`. This is to differentiate between the package of git-svn and the command that is executed.

There are two ways to migrate to Git from Subversion. The first is to import all your history and move on to using Git as your main VCS. The second keeps Subversion around and uses Git's ability to not only import changes from Subversion but also push changes back to it. Both of these are outlined in Figure 10.3.

10.2 Making Sure git-svn Is Available

Git has a tool called git-svn that handles communication with a Subversion repository. Depending on how you installed Git, you may already have git-svn installed. To determine whether you have it installed, run git svn --version:

```
prompt> git svn --version
git-svn version 1.6.0.2 (svn 1.4.4)
```

If your output looks similar to this, you have everything you need and are ready to go. There are two possible error messages you might get instead of the previous output:

- Git complains about SVN not being a command or a fatal error
- An error saying that it can't find SVN/Core.pm

Not a Git Command or Fatal Error

This is a common issue when you install Git through a package manager such as Ubuntu's apt-get or OS X's MacPorts. They break Git into multiple smaller packages to reduce the number of dependencies when installing packages.

To install git-svn on Linux, you need to locate the package that contains the Subversion subcommand for Git. In Ubuntu, this package is aptly named git-svn:

```
prompt> sudo apt-get install git-svn
```

If you installed using MacPorts the way we discussed in Section 2.1, *Installing Git*, on page 15, then you already have git-svn installed. Likewise, if you compiled Git from source, it's already available.

Missing SVN/Core.pm

The other error you might receive is Perl complaining about a missing SVN/Core.pm file. This is caused when you don't have the Perl bindings for Subversion installed.

There are a couple of ways to get the necessary files. The easiest way for most people is to use their package manager.

On Ubuntu, the missing package is called subversion-perl. To install it, type the following:

```
prompt> sudo apt-get install subversion-perl
```

Being the Git: Using Git in a Subversion Company

At a past job, I worked on performance testing and tuning of the company's application. I did a lot of experimentation interspersed with random adjustments to specific areas as they came across my radar. The engineering department used Subversion to track their changes.

My development was anything but linear. I often worked on several different areas during the course of a week. The centralized model with expensive branches and lack of merge tracking didn't work well for me.

Git's cheap branches allowed me to work much more effectively without the mental and physical overhead of maintaining separate copies of the half dozen or so branches I had.

There's another benefit. Following the advice in *Practices of an Agile Developer* (SH06), Git allowed me to share work only when it was ready. If not, I ran the risk of someone seeing some partially completely algorithm change and thinking "Well, if Travis did it this way, it must be good!"

By using Git I could manage multiple branches of code, keeping them all current without manually tracking merges; craft the commits I wanted to push back to our main repository; and commit new code only once it had been proven as more efficient.

If you're on a Mac, the MacPorts package is called subversion-perlbindings:

```
prompt> sudo port install subversion-perlbindings
```

If you use CPAN to keep your Perl libraries up-to-date, you can also install the package directly through it. The package you want to install is SVN::Core:

```
prompt> sudo cpan install SVN::Core
```

10.3 Importing a Subversion Repository

To import a Subversion repository's history into Git, use the git svn clone command to Just like its normal Git counterpart, git svn clone retrieves the entire history of a repository and stores it in your repository.

Beware of CPAN on Mac

I spent two afternoons trying to figure out why MacPorts was telling me I had everything I needed but Git wouldn't recognize it. It turns out I had two versions of the Perl Subversion bindings on my system: an outdated one that was installed by Subversion when I originally set it up on my machine and the newer one on MacPorts.

To make matters worse, before I realized what had happened, I had also installed it via CPAN, so I now had three versions installed! My CPAN one worked, but when I pointed Git to it, another dependency failed. Once I realized that my CPAN library didn't have all the dependencies met, it was a quick fix, but it still took a few hours that I wish I had back.

You do have to tell Git how the repository is structured. If you follow the recommended Subversion repository layout,[1] you can provide the -s. That tells Git to utilize the standard layout.

You can use the -b and -t options if your branches and tags directories are in different locations. Likewise, if your trunk isn't named trunk, you can use the -T option:

```
prompt> git svn clone --prefix svn/ -s svn://svnrepo/sunshine
Initialized empty Git repository in /work/sunshine.git/
Using higher level of URL: svn://svnrepo/sunshine =>
svn://svnrepo/sunshine/
This may take a while on large repositories
branch_from: /tags => /tags/prototype
Found possible branch point:
svn://svnrepo/sunshine/branch/tswicegood-speed
r1 = 305a06a00d6048fe36ee01bb96b7c770cc30317e (trunk)
        A       tests/basic-use-cases.py
r2 = a7f1299c2821f788d64218cc4e366ebe13202105
        A       src/sunshine/__init__.py
        A       src/sunshine/framework.py
... etc., etc. ...
r50 = c534dfb90a8365842af86fde85065d76baca260a (trunk)
Checked out HEAD:
  svn://svnrepo/sunshine r50
```

1. http://svnbook.red-bean.com/en/1.1/ch04s07.html

Shrinking the Size of Your Repository

If you clone a Subversion repository of more than 100 or so commits, you might notice that a lot of disk space has disappeared after the clone is finished.

Just like you would after a few hundred commits, remember to run git gc on a fresh Subversion clone as soon as possible to reduce the amount of disk space taken up.

If it's the first thing you do after you clone the repository, you can safely pass the --aggressive option. This may take a while, though. I've personally seen fourteen-plus CPU hours spent compressing a newly cloned repository with more than 31,000 commits.

Subversion doesn't know how to respond to a request such as "Give me your entire history," so git-svn queries it one revision at a time. For a large repository with tens of thousands of commits, this can take nearly a whole day!

Notice in the earlier git svn clone command that I included a --prefix parameter. That tells git-svn to add a prefix, such as the remote repository names for remote branches, to all the Subversion-based branches. Without adding a prefix, you end up with remote and local branches of the same name. You don't have to add this parameter, but it does make the output of git branch -a much easier to digest.

If old commits aren't important to you, you can use the -r option to specify what revision to start cloning at. Specifying a revision clones the history of that one revision. You have to run another command to pull the rest of the changes. The command git svn rebase is the same command we'll use in the next section to pull changes from our "upstream" Subversion repository after our initial import.

10.4 Keeping Up-to-Date with a Subversion Repository

Whether you are communicating with an active Subversion repository or you used git svn clone -r ... to make your initial clone, you can pull changes from your Subversion repository in two ways.

Joe Asks...

What's with That Error?

If you cloned a project within a repository that isn't present in the oldest commit, you might see errors similar to these:

```
W: Ignoring error from SVN, path probably does
not exist: (175002): RA layer request failed:
REPORT request failed on '/test/!svn/bc/100':
REPORT of '/test/!svn/bc/100': Could not read
chunk size: Secure connection truncated
(svn://svnrepo)
W: Do not be alarmed at the above message
git-svn is just searching aggressively for
old history.
```

As the second warning (the lines that start with W:) says, don't worry. When git-svn tries to clone your Subversion repository, it starts at the oldest revision it can access and keeps moving forward until it can find a revision that contains the code you've referenced.

The warning is telling you is that it couldn't find the code at the oldest revision it requested. It continues through the history until it finds the revision where the project you're trying to clone first exists.

The first is git svn fetch. It pulls all the remote changes into their remote branch but doesn't try to merge them into your local branch. This is also the command you use to grab new branches from Subversion.

The second, and the one that gets more use, is git svn rebase. It works like git svn fetch followed by git rebase. It pulls all the commits from your upstream Subversion repository and then rebases your current branch against the remote branch.

Just like with git rebase, if you have a local commit that has been applied on Subversion, it will not apply that patch again when rebasing. Also, like its regular Git counterpart, git svn rebase can't run when there are uncommitted changes in your working tree.

Alternative to Cloning a Subversion Repository

Cloning a Subversion repository can be a time-consuming process. I've cloned large repositories that have taken more than twenty CPU hours. If you're trying to clone a large existing repository, ask around for a *bootstrap repository* before you start cloning yourself.

A bootstrap repository is a tarball of a Git repository that has been cloned from the Subversion repository you want to track. In the open source community, bootstrap repositories are normally updated every week or so.

Using a bootstrap repository, all you have to do is type `git svn rebase` to grab all the changes since the last time the bootstrap was updated. That's a lot faster than cloning an entire history!

10.5 Pushing Changes to SVN

We've covered everything you need to know if you're migrating to Git and leaving your Subversion repository behind. Share your newly created repository, and skip this section.

One of the benefits of Git over other popular DVCSs, however, is its ability to continue to not only pull but also *push* changes back to Subversion.

The command to push changes back to Subversion is `git svn dcommit`. It takes each of the commits you've made locally and commits them back to your Subversion repository, one by one.

During this process, it rebases your copy so each of your local commit reflects the information from the Subversion server. Just like `git svn rebase`, this is to make it easier for git-svn to figure out what it has already synced.

You can use the `-n` option to tell Git you want to do a "dry run." In this mode, it looks through your history and lists all the commits it would send to the Subversion repository.

10.6 Importing from CVS

If you're coming to Git from CVS, there are some hurdles you must jump over compared to Subversion. In fact, the most reliable method for converting a CVS repository to Git is to convert it to a Subversion repository first using the cvs2svn command.[2] cvs2svn is a tool for converting a CVS repository to a Subversion repository.

Git ships with a tool for importing CVS repositories called git cvsimport. Since the cvs2svn command is much more stable to a Git repository, we'll focus on it.

To start with, you need to get revision control system (RCS) files from your CVS repository. Once you have those, you need to convert them to an SVN dump file using the cvs2svn tool:

```
prompt> cd /path/to/cvs-rcs-files
prompt> cvs2svn --dumpfile=svndump
```

Creating the dump file allows you to filter out any unnecessary data by using tools such as svndumpfilter.[3] With your new svndump prepared, now you need to create a Subversion repository to import it into. You can do this by using the svnadmin create command:

```
prompt> cd ..
prompt> svnadmin create ./tmpsvn
prompt> svnadmin load ./tmpsvn < /path/to/cvs-rcs-files/svndump
```

Assuming there were no problems loading the history into your tmpsvn repository, now you're ready to import that into Git. The process is the same as the one covered in Section 10.1, *Communicating with SVN*, on page 131:

```
prompt> git svn clone file:///path/to/tmpsvn
```

Now you know how to get your history out of Subversion and CVS and into Git. You can even treat Subversion like a shared upstream repository, pushing changes back to it.

In the next chapter, you'll learn how to manage upstream Git repositories through Gitosis.

---

2. You can download this in source form directly from http://cvs2svn.tigris.org/, or you can get it from your favorite package manager in Linux or MacPorts in OS X.

3. http://svnbook.red-bean.com/en/1.1/ch05s03.html#svn-ch-5-sect-3.1.3

Chapter 11

Running a Git Server with Gitosis

Gitosis is a tool that shows off the brilliance of Git. Not only is Git a distributed version control system, but it is a platform for building other applications that depend on a file system and can benefit from versioning.

More specifically, Gitosis is a tool for managing a remote Git server and its repositories. It does this by using a Git repository to store its configuration. All you have to do if you need to update the configuration of the server is push that new configuration to the Gitosis repository.

It manages this by taking advantage of the hook scripts, located in the .git/hooks/ directory. Hook scripts execute at certain events such as before a commit (the pre-commit script) or right after a commit (post-commit).

Gitosis uses these scripts to update the configuration files for the repositories you create. It handles things such as creating the empty repository and who has access to read or write to the repository for you.

Gitosis is still a fairly new project, so you have to get your hands a little dirty working under the hood to get it installed and configured. The steps required to install Gitosis are as follows:

1. Making sure dependencies are met
2. Installing Gitosis
3. Configuring the server for Gitosis
4. Creating administrator credentials
5. Initializing Gitosis
6. Configuring Gitosis

If you're not familiar with running daemons on your server, this chapter might not be for you. The topics we're covering, although straightforward, fall to the more complex end of the spectrum.

Don't fret if setting up servers isn't your thing; you have a couple of options. You can try to enlist the help of a sysadmin buddy by bribing, err, paying him to help you out. This chapter will make perfect sense to him.

Or, if your social circle is lacking anyone who can work their sysadmin magic for you, you can also look to external hosting services. GitHub and Gitorious both offer free hosting. I talk more about these in Section B.3, *Git Repository Hosting*, on page 169.

11.1 Making Sure Dependencies Are Met

Gitosis has a few dependencies. First, since it is written in Python, you will need to have that installed on your system. Python is pretty popular, so it may already be installed on your system. The easiest way to check is to run the following command from the command prompt:

```
prompt> python --version
Python 2.5.1
```

If Python is installed on your system, you will get a response similar to the one shown here, but the version number may be different depending on which version of Python you have installed.

You also need the EasyInstall package from the Python Enterprise Application Kit (PEAK). EasyInstall is a package that helps developers install Python-based applications and handle dependencies. It is a popular package, so you may already have it installed on your system. You can check by running the following from the command line:

```
prompt> python -c "import setuptools"
```

There is no output if EasyInstall and its setuptools module are available. If you get a warning similar to the following one, you will need to install EasyInstall. Check your operation system's documentation for information on how to install EasyInstall, or follow the instructions on its website.[1]

```
prompt> python -c "import setuptools"
Traceback (most recent call last):
  File "<stdin>", line 1, in <module>
ImportError: No module named setuptools
```

1. http://peak.telecommunity.com/DevCenter/EasyInstall

11.2 Installing Gitosis

Gitosis is still in active development, so you have to install it from its source code. You can get its source code directly from its Git repository by cloning it:

```
prompt> git clone git://eagain.net/gitosis
Initialized empty Git repository in /work/gitosis/.git/
remote: Counting objects: 599, done.
remote: Compressing objects: 100% (168/168), done.
remote: Total 599 (delta 422), reused 599 (delta 422)
Receiving objects: 100% (599/599), 92.57 KiB | 59 KiB/s, done.
Resolving deltas: 100% (422/422), done.
```

Now you have a copy of the source code located in the gitosis directory. To install Gitosis, change into that directory, and run the setup.py file like this:

```
prompt> cd gitosis
prompt> sudo python setup.py install
running install
... a few hundred more lines of output ...
```

Now that Gitosis is installed, you need to set up a user on your server that Gitosis can use. To do that, you have to create the credentials for your user.

11.3 Creating Administrator Credentials

You must create a SSH public key for your admin user on Gitosis. A SSH public key is used by SSH to verify your connection instead of using a password.

If you already have a public key that you use with SSH, you can use that now instead of creating a new one. If not, you will need to create a key. Keys can be created from the command line by using the ssh-keygen command.

You need this command on your local computer, the one you use to connect to your server running Gitosis. You can generate your key by running the following from the command line:

```
prompt> ssh-keygen -t rsa
```

The program will prompt you for the location where you want to store the new key. The default location is fine, so hit the Enter key to accept it. It will then ask for your passphrase. Your passphrase is required in order to use the key you are generating. Just like a normal password, choose this carefully, and make sure you don't give it to anyone.

The ssh-keygen program creates your key and gives you some information about the new key. If you left the location and name at their default values, you now have a public key located in this location:

/home/<username>/.ssh/id_rsa.pub

Copy this file to your server. You're going to be using it shortly when you initialize Gitosis.

11.4 Configuring the Server for Gitosis

Gitosis requires two things in order to run on your server. It must have its own user on the server and a directory to store all your repositories.

Each operating system has a slightly different way for adding new users. In most Linux distributions, you can use the adduser command.

Gitosis needs a new user on the system. Their home directory is where Gitosis stores its configuration values and its repositories. You can specify the home directory on most Linux systems by adding --home /path/to/home.

The home path can be located anywhere on the system that you want. The convention within Gitosis is to put it in /srv/example.com/git—changing *example.com* out for your domain—but that isn't required.

You can name this user whatever you would like, but I'm going with git. If you use something else, substitute the username in the commands in the rest of this chapter with your username.

```
prompt> sudo adduser --shell /bin/sh \
                     --group \
                     --disabled-password \
                     --home /srv/example.com/git
                     git
```

For those familiar with adduser, this command will be self-explanatory. It creates a user named git that has their home set to /srv/example.com/git, disables logging in with a password, adds a git group, and sets their shell to /bin/sh.

With the user set up and credentials already created, now you need to initialize Gitosis.

11.5 Initializing Gitosis

Gitosis comes with a program, gitosis-init, to handle initialization. gitosis-init doesn't require any options, but it must be run as the user you created in the previous section. If you used the recommended git user, your init command looks like this:

```
prompt> sudo -H -u git gitosis-init < /path/to/id_rsa.pub
Initialized empty Git repository in
    /srv/example.com/repositories/gitosis-admin.git/
Reinitialized existing Git repository in
    /srv/example.com/repositories/gitosis-admin.git/
```

This initializes Gitosis and its repository. All that's left now is the configuration. If you got an OSError exception, continue reading this section. Otherwise, you can skip ahead.

If you've installed Git in a location that's not in your normal $PATH, you'll get this error instead of the successful output shown previously. This is because the gitosis-init command can't find Git.

To fix this, you need to make sure the Git commands are available to the git user. You can do this by modifying $PATH variable for the user Gitosis is running as, or you can make sure that the Git commands are available to the user by adding a symbolic link to the git binary in one of the directories in the Gitosis user's $PATH.

11.6 Configuring Gitosis

Now you need to clone Gitosis's configuration repository. It contains all the configuration values you need to manage your new repositories. You must clone it from the computer where you generated the SSH public key. That's the only one that Gitosis knows about right now.

If your server's domain name was example.com, your clone command would look something like this:

```
prompt> git clone git@example.com:gitosis-admin.git
Initialized empty Git repository in /work/gitosis-admin/.git/
remote: Counting objects: 5, done.
remote: Compressing objects: 100% (4/4), done.
remote: Total 5 (delta 1), reused 5 (delta 1)
Receiving objects: 100% (5/5), done.
Resolving deltas: 100% (1/1), done.
```

There is a gitosis.conf file and a keydir/ directory in your newly cloned repository.

gitosis.conf is a simple INI-style file. Its sections are denoted by brackets, and its values have a name, an =, and the value. The default configuration looks something like this:

```
[gitosis]

[group gitosis-admin]
writable = gitosis-admin
members = travis
```

The part that's interesting here is the block after [group gitosis-admin]. The first line specifies that this group can write to the gitosis-admin repository. The second line specifies the users—or in this case the user—that are part of this group.

The members field is a space-separated field. Each entry refers to a file in the keydir directory of the same name with a .pub extension. For example, the key for my user is located in keydir/travis.pub.

To add a new user, you need their public SSH key. Each developer who wants access to your repository needs to generate their key on their computer. It can be generated using the command you used earlier, but it has to be done on their computer. Each key is specific to a particular computer.

Once you have a copy of their public key, add it to the keydir/ directory, named with the name you want to use for them, and then add that name to the repositories you want to give them access to. Once you've committed those changes to your local repository, you need to push it to the Gitosis server with a quick git push command.

11.7 Adding New Repositories

The initial configuration that Gitosis creates has one configuration repository, but you can manage as many repositories as you like. If you want to, you can add new writable lines to the gitosis-admin group, but that means everyone with access to your repositories has access to change Gitosis' configuration. A more secure solution is to create two groups: one for administrators and another for normal developers.

Here's a sample configuration:

```
[gitosis]

[group gitosis-admin]
writable = gitosis-admin
members = travis
```

```
[group team]
writable = mysite
members = travis susannah
```

Recognize the first [group] from earlier? This configuration adds a new group called team and says that the team members can write to the mysite repository; then it gives write access to users travis and susannah.

For each new repository you want to create, add a new writable line with that repository's name. Once again, commit your changes and push them to your server. After pushing the changes, you can add content to your new remote repository.

You can send content to your new remote repository from any local Git repository. Your local repository has to have at least one commit so there is something to send, though. From the working tree of that repository, execute the following command to add a remote repository to your configuration:

```
prompt> git remote add origin git@example.com:mysite.git
```

That adds the mysite remote repository to your local repository's configuration as its origin repository. Obviously, you need to swap out example.com with whatever your server's domain name is and mysite.git with the name of your repository.

Now all that's left is to push the contents of your local repository to the remote repository. That's a simple enough command, but remember you have to specify the branch you want to push to since it doesn't exist on your remote repository yet:

```
prompt> git push origin master
Initialized empty Git repository in
    /srv/example.com/git/repositories/mysite.git/
Counting objects: 3, done.
Writing objects: 100% (3/3), 214 bytes, done.
Total 3 (delta 0), reused 0 (delta 0)
To git@example.com:test.git
 * [new branch]      master -> master
```

Now you're set. Other users who have access can clone your repository and push changes to it too if you gave them permission to write to the repository.

On an open source project, your repository needs to be accessible by the public at large. You might even need to expose your repository on your local VPN to everyone in the company, but you don't need to keep track of who is logging in to read its contents.

You can set up your repository to allow anonymous read-only access using git daemon, which we'll cover next.

11.8 Setting Up a Public Repository

The one last thing you might need to do is set up the read-only portion of your repository. You have to do this only if you want to share your work with other developers without having to set up a user for them. This is most common in open source development where anyone can read from the repository.

Setting this up requires two steps. First, you have to configure your repository for sharing with Gitosis. Second, you have to run git daemon to respond to the requests.

To configure Gitosis, you need to edit the gitosis.conf name from earlier. This time, add a new section called repo with the name of your repository. For example, if your repository were called web, you would add this:

```
[repo web]
```

That's the INI setting for creating the new section. It tells the configuration that everything that comes after it is part of that section. Now you need to add a line that says daemon = yes so git daemon knows this repository can be read. Your new section should look like this:

```
[repo web]
daemon = yes
```

That's all there is to the configuration step. Commit your changes, and push them to your server. Now you need to set git daemon.

git daemon needs to be run as your git user that you created earlier. The easiest way to do that is by using sudo -u git to prefix your command.

Other than that, the only parameter that git daemon needs is --base-path. That tells it where to look for your repositories. Following the configuration that we've used so far, this is located in /srv/example.com/repositories.

The actual command to run git daemon looks like this:

```
prompt> sudo -u git git daemon \
        --base-path /srv/example.com/repositories/
```

You can test that this works by cloning one of your read-only repositories. Using the web repository, the clone command is as follows:

```
prompt> git clone git://example.com/web.git
```

Now you're set. The git daemon command that you executed will run only as long as that user is logged in. It also doesn't run every time your server boots up. Each operating system handles that a little differently.

I use nohup when I want to run git daemon even after I log out of my server, but I don't need it to start up when I reboot my server. The command I use looks something like this:

```
prompt> nohup sudo -u git git daemon \
        --base-path /srv/example.com/repositories &
```

The final & suffix detaches it from the current session, and the nohup prefix detaches it from the current user.

A final note: Gitosis is stable but still relatively new, just like Git. I have used it exclusively to manage my Git repositories for the better part of a year and never had any issues with its reliability.

It is tightly coupled with Git, however, so there may be incompatibility issues between different versions of Git. I ran into one that was caused by a change in Git from version 1.5.*x* to 1.6.0. It has already been fixed, but there's always the possibility that something like that will pop up.

If you run into any issues installing Gitosis, you can try the book's forums,[2] or if IRC is more your thing, the #git channel on Freenode always has a few people with experience including usually Tv, the developer of Gitosis.

11.9 Closing Thoughts

This brings us to the end of the book. There's some additional information in a few appendixes. In Appendix A, on page 155, you'll find recipes for the common tasks in Git. Consider it your Git cookbook. In Appendix B, on page 165, you'll find information on a few of the extra tools and resources available to you as a Git user. The book finishes up with Appendix C, on page 173. It lists all the other books referenced throughout this book.

2. http://forums.pragprog.com/forums/64

I hope you've enjoyed reading this book as much as I have enjoyed writing it. It has been a great learning experience and a lot of fun, and I hope that has come through in the book. If you have any questions, feel free to stop by the book's forum[3] and drop me a line.

3. http://forums.pragprog.com/forums/64

Part IV

Appendixes

Appendix A

Git Command Quick Reference

This appendix is your quick reference for how to perform common Git tasks. Each section focuses on one type of task.

This appendix is light on content and heavy on commands. If you're skipping ahead and aren't familiar with the concepts of Git, now would be a good time to flip through Chapter 1, *Version Control the Git Way*, on page 3.

A.1 Setup and Initialization

Before you start working with Git, you have to configure it. Before you can start working on a new project, you have to initialize it. This section covers commands related to the initial configuration and setup of Git.

Configure Global Username/Email

```
prompt> git config --global user.name "Your Name"
prompt> git config --global user.email "you@example.com"
```

Configure Username/Email for a Specific Repository

Note: You can set your username and email address on a per-repository basis. This allows you to use a different name and/or email address for different projects.

```
prompt> cd /path/to/repo
prompt> git config user.name "Your Name"
prompt> git config user.email "you@example.com"
```

Turn Color On in Git's Output

```
prompt> git config --global color.ui "auto"
```

Initialize a New Repository

```
prompt> mkdir /path/to/repo
prompt> cd /path/to/repo
prompt> git init
Initialized empty Git repository in /path/to/repo/.git/
prompt>
... create file(s) for first commit ...
prompt> git add .
prompt> git commit -m 'initial import'
Created initial commit bdebe5c: initial import
 1 files changed, 1 insertions(+), 0 deletions(-)
 create mode 100644 <some file>
```

Clone a Repository

```
prompt> git clone <repository url>
Initialize repo/.git
Initialized empty Git repository in /work/<remote repository>/.git/
```

Add Git to an Existing Directory

```
prompt> cd /path/to/existing/directory
prompt> git init
Initialized empty Git repository in /path/to/existing/directory/.git/
prompt> git add .
prompt> git commit -m "initial import of some project"
```

Add a New Remote Repository

```
... from within the repository directory ...
prompt> git remote add <remote repository> <repository url>
```

A.2 Normal Usage

You use these commands doing normal, day-to-day activities. These are your bread-and-butter commands, the ones we covered in Chapter 4, *Adding and Committing: Git Basics*, on page 41.

Add a New File or Stage an Existing File and Commit

```
prompt> git add <some file>
prompt> git commit -m "<some message>"
```

Stage a Partial File

Note: [...] indicates optional parameters.

```
prompt> git add -p [<some file> [<some file> [and so on]]]
... select hunks to commit ...
```

Add Files via Git's Interactive Add Mode

```
prompt> git add -i
```

Stage Changes to Modified, Tracked Files

```
prompt> git add -u [<some path> [<some path>]]
```

Commit Changes to All Modified, Tracked Files

```
prompt> git commit -m "<some message>" -a
```

Revert Changes in a Working Tree

```
prompt> git checkout HEAD <some file> [<some file>]
```

Reset Staged Changes That Haven't Been Committed

```
prompt> git reset HEAD <some file> [<some file>]
```

Fix the Last Commit

```
... make whatever changes and stage them ...
prompt> git commit -m "<some message>" --amend
```

Amend the Previous Commit and Reuse a Commit Message

```
prompt> git commit -C HEAD --amend
```

A.3 Branches

Branches are one of Git's strongest points. This section covers commands related to all aspects of branches. You can find more details in Chapter 5, *Understanding and Using Branches*, on page 55.

Show Local Branches

```
prompt> git branch
```

Show Just Remote Branches

```
prompt> git branch -r
```

Show All Local and Remote Branches

```
prompt> git branch -a
```

Create a New Branch from the Current Branch

```
prompt> git branch <new branch>
```

Check Out Another Branch

```
prompt> git checkout <some branch>
```

Create a New Branch from the Current Branch and Check It Out

```
prompt> git checkout -b <new branch>
```

Create a Branch from Another Starting Point

You can create a branch from any start point within the history of the repository. The start point can be another branch, a commit name, or a tag.

```
prompt> git branch <new branch> <start point>
```

Overwrite the Existing Branch with a New Branch

```
prompt> git branch -f <some existing branch> [<start point>]
```

Move or Rename a Branch

...only if *<new branch>* does *not* exist

```
prompt> git checkout -m <existing branch name> <new branch name>
```

...overwriting any existing branch

```
prompt> git checkout -M <existing branch name> <new branch name>
```

Merge Another Branch into the Current Branch

```
prompt> git merge <some branch>
```

Merge but Don't Commit

```
prompt> git merge --no-commit <some branch>
```

Cherry-Pick Commit

```
prompt> git cherry-pick <commit name>
```

Cherry-Pick, but Don't Commit

```
prompt> git cherry-pick -n <commit name>
```

Squash One Branch's History into Another

```
prompt> git merge --squash <some branch>
```

Delete a Branch

...only if branch has been merged into current branch

```
prompt> git branch -d <branch to delete>
```

...even if branch has not been merged into current branch

```
prompt> git branch -D <branch to delete>
```

A.4 History

These commands show you your history, including where your code has been, who did what and when, changes, and statistics. Many of these commands are covered in more detail in Chapter 6, *Working with Git's History*, on page 71.

Show All History

```
prompt> git log
```

Display Log with Patch Showing Change

```
prompt> git log -p
```

Limit Log to Show One Entry

```
prompt> git log -1
```

Limit Log to Show Twenty Entries and Patches

```
prompt> git log -20 -p
```

Show Commits from Past Six Hours

```
prompt> git log --since="6 hours"
```

Show Commits Older Than Two Days

```
prompt> git log --before="2 days"
```

Show Log for Single Commit Three Commits Prior to HEAD

```
prompt> git log -1 HEAD~3
```

Or...

```
prompt> git log -1 HEAD^^^
```

Or...

```
prompt> git log -1 HEAD~1^^
```

Show Commits Between Two Points

<start point> and <end point> in the following example can be a commit, branch, or tag name. You can also mix different names.

```
prompt> git log <start point>...<end point>
```

Show Log History as One-Liners

```
prompt> git log --pretty=oneline
```

Show Stats of Affected Lines for Each Line Entry

```
prompt> git log --stat
```

Show Status of Files Touched by a Commit

```
prompt> git log --name-status
```

Show the Differences Between the Current Working Tree and the Index

```
prompt> git diff
```

Show the Differences Between the Index and the Repository

```
prompt> git diff --cached
```

Show the Differences Between the Working Tree and the Repository

```
prompt> git diff HEAD
```

Show the Differences Between the Working Tree and the Previous Point in Repository

<start point> can be a commit, branch, or tag name.

```
prompt> git diff <start point>
```

Show the Differences Between Two Points in a Repository

```
prompt> git diff <start point> <end point>
```

Show Stats from Differences

```
prompt> git diff --stat <start point> [<end point>]
```

Annotate a File with Commit Information

```
prompt> git blame <some file>
```

Annotate File and Show Copy and Paste and Line Movement Within File

```
prompt> git blame -M <some file>
```

Annotate File, Show Line Movement and Original File

```
prompt> git blame -C -C <some file>
```

Show Copy and Paste Within the Log

```
prompt> git log -C -C -p -1 <some point>
```

A.5 Remote Repositories

You collaborate with other developers by using remote repositories to share your work and interact with others' work. This section covers those commands, many of which are covered in Chapter 7, *Working with Remote Repositories*, on page 91.

Clone a Repository

```
prompt> git clone <some repository>
```

Clone a Repository but Download Only the Last 200 Commits

```
prompt> git clone --depth 200 <some repository>
```

Add a New Named Remote Repository

```
prompt> git remote add <remote repository> <repository url>
```

Show All Remote Branches

```
prompt> git branch -r
```

Create a Local Branch from a Remote Branch

```
prompt> git branch <new branch> <remote branch>
```

Create a Local Branch from a Remote Tag

```
prompt> git branch <new branch> <remote tag>
```

Fetch Changes from Origin Repository, but Do Not Merge into Local Branch

```
prompt> git fetch
```

Fetch Changes from a Remote Repository Other Than Origin, but Do Not Merge

```
prompt> git fetch <remote repository>
```

Fetch Changes from a Remote Repository and Merge into Current Branch

```
prompt> git pull <remote repository>
```

Fetch Changes from Origin Repository and Merge into Current Branch

```
prompt> git pull
```

Push Local Branch to Remote Branch

```
prompt> git push <remote repository> <local branch>:<remote branch>
```

Push Local Branch to Remote Branch of Same Name

```
prompt> git push <remote repository> <local branch>
```

Push New Local Branch to Remote Repository

```
prompt> git push <remote repository> <local branch>
```

Push Local Changes to Origin Repository

This pushes only those branches that are already present in the origin repository. To push a new branch, you must use the git push <repository name> <local branch> syntax.

```
prompt> git push
```

Delete a Remote Branch

```
prompt> git push <remote repository> :<remote branch>
```

Remove Any Stale Remote Branches

```
prompt> git remote prune <remote repository>
```

Remove a Remote Repository and Any Associated Branches

```
prompt> git remote rm <remote repository>
```

A.6 Git to SVN Bridge

The ability to receive and send commits to and from a Subversion repository is one of the many finishing touches that sets Git apart from all the other DVCSs. These are a few of the more common commands used when working with a remote SVN repository. You can find out more about them in Chapter 10, *Migrating to Git*, on page 131.

Clone an Entire SVN Repository

```
prompt> git svn clone <svn repository>
```

Clone an Entire SVN Repository Using Standard Layout

Use this if you are cloning a repository that uses the standard trunk, branches, and tags repository structure:

```
prompt> git svn clone -s <svn repository>
```

Clone an Entire SVN Repository with Nonstandard Layout

```
prompt> git svn clone -T <trunk path> \
    -b <branch path> \
    -t <tag path> \
    <svn repository>
```

Clone an SVN Repository with Standard Layout at Revision 2321

```
prompt> git svn clone -s -r 2321
```

Clone SVN Repository with Standard Layout and Add Prefix to All Remote Branches

```
prompt> git svn clone -s --prefix svn/ <svn repository>
```

Update from Upstream SVN Repository and Rebase

```
prompt> git svn rebase
```

Push Commits Back to Upstream SVN Repository

```
prompt> git svn dcommit
```

View List of Commits That Would Be Pushed Upstream

```
prompt> git svn dcommit -n
```

View SVN Log of Repository

```
prompt> git svn log
```

View SVN Blame for a File

```
prompt> git svn blame <some file>
```

Appendix B

Other Resources and Tools

Git is a growing and maturing open source project. This book outlines the core tools you need to work with Git daily, but you can access a whole host of other tools and resources as you work to get the most out of Git.

B.1 Extras Bundled with Git

Git has many great tools that are packaged directly with it. Installing it through a package system such as apt-get or MacPorts means you might have to install these tools separately.

gitk

Arguably one of the most useful tools in Git, gitk visualizes your repository's history, showing you how all the various branches come together in the history.

gitk is billed as the "original Tcl/Tk GUI for browsing the history of a Git repository." It requires Tcl/Tk, which is already installed on many Linux and Mac computers.

The configuration needs a little tweaking to look decent on a Mac. You can add configuration values to the .gitk file in your home directory to customize the interface. I like my development interfaces to all use the same font at the same size—Panic Sans at 11 points.[1]

1. Panic Sans is part of the Coda package, which is available online at http://www.panic.com/coda.

My .gitk file looks like this:

```
set mainfont {{Panic Sans} 11}
set textfont {{Panic Sans} 11}
set uifont {{Panic Sans} 11 bold}
```

git-gui

git-gui provides an interface to the basic commands you need when working with a repository. You can use it to view files that are not being tracked, changed files, and what is staged. It also lets you stage changes and make commits.

It is platform independent, so you can use it in any operating system, but the cross-platform capabilities mean it doesn't integrate as smoothly with your operating system the way tools such as Tortoise SVN/CVS do.

gitweb

gitweb is a web front end to Git repositories. You may have seen it in action at http://git.kernel.org or http://repo.or.cz. gitweb incorporates every feature you need to view your repository in a web interface.

It is bundled with Git's source code in the gitweb directory. Full information on how to install it and how to configure it is available in the INSTALL and README files in that directory.

B.2 Third-Party Tools

More tools are being made for Git every day. This section highlights a few of the standout tools. All of these are currently maintained outside the official Git distribution, but many are created by developers who also contribute to Git.

GitX

GitX is a native OS X clone of gitk. It performs the same functions, except it looks like a native OS X application. You can view any branch one at a time or all the branches at once like with gitk. Its latest version includes the ability to create commits, similar to git-gui.

It is fairly new with the first commit being made in June 2008, but it was already up to its fourth stable release—0.4—by early fall of 2008. It is hosted on GitHub, where you can download the latest build and get information on building it from source.

http://gitx.frim.nl/

Komodo IDE

ActiveState announced that it's integrating support for several DVCSs including Git in the 5.0 release of the Komodo IDE. Komodo is an integrated development environment geared toward scripting languages and web development. It is built on Mozilla 1.9, the same branch of Mozilla that Firefox 3 is written on.

ActiveState released the first alpha version of Komodo IDE version 5.0 in August 2008. The current plan is to have the stable release out sometime in the fall of 2008. You can obtain information about the latest version of the Komodo IDE from its website.

http://www.activestate.com/Products/komodo_ide/

Eclipse Git Plug-In

Eclipse is a popular cross-browser IDE written in Java. It has support for every major programming language and runs on any platform that Java runs on. There is a Git plug-in that allows you to use Git directly inside the IDE.

Features include the ability to commit, amend commits, view diffs, and visualize the repository history graphically. You can find more information, including download information, on the project's wiki page.

http://git.or.cz/gitwiki/EclipsePlugin

TextMate Git Bundle

TextMate bills itself as "the missing editor for Mac OS X." Its excellent support for scripting languages and ease of use make it popular with developers working on OS X.[2]

There is a Git Bundle for TextMate that allows you to work with Git directly inside TextMate. You can get the bundle and more information about how to install it from the project website on Gitorious.

http://gitorious.org/projects/git-tmbundle

VCSCommand

Word of caution—I'm a Vim user. I used MacVim for nearly all the writing of this book, so this review might be slanted.

---

2. *TextMate: Power Editing for the Mac* [Gra07] is also available from the Pragmatic Bookshelf if you're interested in learning more about TextMate.

VCSCommand is a plug-in for the wildly popular and battle-tested Vim editor. Combine it with a few shortcuts in your .vimrc file, and you're set to take on the most challenging programming projects on any platform.

Too over the top? OK, I'll back it down a notch. Vim is an editor that has been ported to every major platform. It's even available on a "jailbroken" iPhone. Vim, or its predecessor vi, is available on nearly every Linux box, so there's a good chance it's available when editing code on a Linux box.

VCSCommand lets you interact with several VCS directly through Vim. It currently supports CVS, Subversion, and Git. It's written in Python so it requires the Python bindings for Vim. You can get more information about VCSCommand from its listing on the Vim Scripts site.

http://www.vim.org/scripts/script.php?script_id=90

GitNub

GitNub describes itself as a gitk-like tool that looks like it belongs on a Mac. It provides basic viewing of history and has integration with GitHub's timeline viewer if your repository is hosted on GitHub.

You have to build GitNub from source. It requires Ruby and RubyCocoa along with Leopard. You can get more information and the URL to clone it from its listing on GitHub.

http://github.com/Caged/gitnub

TicGit

Ticket-tracking systems are how many teams keep track of who is working on what. These introduce a centralized system into your distributed tool set. TicGit lets you disconnect again with a simple distributed ticket system within Git.

TicGit stores all your ticket information in a branch inside your repository, so whoever clones your repository also has a copy of the tickets associated with it. The only interface right now is through the command line, but a web interface is planned.

You can download the latest and get an introduction on how to interact with TicGit on the TicGit website.

http://github.com/schacon/ticgit/wikis

git-sh

Reading this book, you no doubt noticed that git is typed a lot. git-sh removes the need to type git before every command in Git—you can type checkout when you want to check out or commit when you're ready to commit changes.

It does this by launching a customized shell and creating aliases for all the Git commands. It also adds the name of your current repository and the branch you're on to your command prompt so you don't have to type git branch to see your current branch. The code and installation instructions are available on its GitHub site.

http://github.com/rtomayko/git-sh

B.3 Git Repository Hosting

There are several repository hosting services if you don't want to run your own Git server. These range from services that allow only open source to commercial paid hosting. This section covers a few of the most notable services.

repo.or.cz

The original free Git hosting site, repo.or.cz offers free Git repository hosting to open source projects. It is limited to open source only, but it houses a large collection of repositories.

It is based around the Gitweb package, so the interface should be familiar to those who have set up Gitweb for their repositories. The URL is http://repo.or.cz.

GitHub

GitHub is familiar to nearly everyone who has viewed a Git repository of an open source project. It is the hosting provider used for this book's repositories, it hosts the Rails repository, and it is home to many of the tools listed in this appendix.

It offers several unique features. In particular, it adds a social aspect to software development by allowing people to track who has forked a project. Its tracking makes it easy for you to see all the developers who are contributing code to a project.

GitHub is free for open source projects, but it also offers private hosting for a fee for companies that want to use GitHub to manage their own private projects. You can get more information and sign up by visiting its website.

http://github.com

Gitorious

Gitorious is another free Git hosting provider. The user interface is similar to GitHub, and it offers some similar features, with two exceptions:

- There is no hosting of private repositories on Gitorious.
- The source code for Gitorious is available under the Affero General Public License, which is similar to the GPL with one addition. You must release the source code from any service that uses the AGPL.

http://gitorious.org

B.4 Online Resources

A ton of information about Git is available online. This section highlights the main stops for information online.

git.or.cz

The source for all things Git is the main Git website, has links to the latest source code, user documentation, wiki, and many of the projects related to Git.

git.or.cz

Git Manual

The user's manual is the definitive source on how to do everything in Git. It lists all the commands and their options. Thanks to the community surrounding Git, the documentation is becoming stronger everyday. Every time you run `git --help <some command>`, you're accessing the user manual.

The entire command manual is available online as well.

http://www.kernel.org/pub/software/scm/git/docs/

Git Mailing List

Like many open source projects, a lot of the interaction amongst the developers and the community happens on the mailing list.

git@vger.kernel.org

You can subscribe to the mailing list by sending an email with "subscribe git" in the body of the message to the following address:

majordomo@vger.kernel.org

#git IRC channel

Git has an active community on IRC—#git on Freenode. There is always someone willing to answer questions, from basic to advanced.

From time to time, I'm also on the IRC channel. I'm the ever creatively named tswicegood, so say "Hi" if you see me in the channel.

Pragmatic Version Control Using Git Forums

Lastly, I would be remiss if I didn't mention the book's forums.

http://forums.pragprog.com/forums/64

I keep an eye on the forums regularly, and though most of the discussion so far has been related to the book, I hope they turn into a place where people can come for help when they're looking to answers to their Git questions.

Appendix C

Bibliography

[FBB+99] Martin Fowler, Kent Beck, John Brant, William Opdyke, and Don Roberts. *Refactoring: Improving the Design of Existing Code.* Addison Wesley Longman, Reading, MA, 1999.

[Fri97] Jeffrey E. F. Friedl. *Mastering Regular Expressions.* O'Reilly & Associates, Inc, Sebastopol, CA, 1997.

[Gra07] James Edward Gray II. *TextMate: Power Editing for the Mac.* The Pragmatic Programmers, LLC, Raleigh, NC, and Dallas, TX, 2007.

[Hun08] Andy Hunt. *Pragmatic Thinking & Learning: Refactor Your Wetware.* The Pragmatic Programmers, LLC, Raleigh, NC, and Dallas, TX, 2008.

[SH06] Venkat Subramaniam and Andy Hunt. *Practices of an Agile Developer: Working in the Real World.* The Pragmatic Programmers, LLC, Raleigh, NC, and Dallas, TX, 2006.

Index

A

B

C

D

E

F

G

S

T

U

V

W

Web 2.0

Welcome to the Web, version 2.0. You need some help to tame the wild technologies out there. Start with *Prototype and script.aculo.us*, a book about two libraries that will make your JavaScript life much easier.

See how to reach the largest possible web audience with *The Accessible Web*.

Prototype and script.aculo.us

Tired of getting swamped in the nitty-gritty of cross-browser, Web 2.0–grade JavaScript? Get back in the game with Prototype and script.aculo.us, two extremely popular JavaScript libraries that make it a walk in the park. Be it Ajax, drag and drop, autocompletion, advanced visual effects, or many other great features, all you need is to write one or two lines of script that look so good they could almost pass for Ruby code!

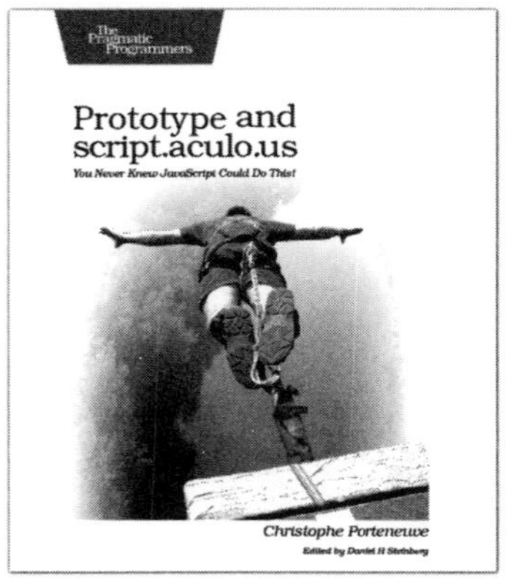

Prototype and script.aculo.us: You never knew JavaScript could do this!
Christophe Porteneuve
(330 pages) ISBN: 1-934356-01-8. $34.95
http://pragprog.com/titles/cppsu

Design Accessible Web Sites

The 2000 U.S. Census revealed that 12% of the population is severely disabled. Sometime in the next two decades, one in five Americans will be older than 65. Section 508 of the Americans with Disabilities Act requires your website to provide *equivalent access* to all potential users. But beyond the law, it is both good manners and good business to make your site accessible to everyone. This book shows you how to design sites that excel for all audiences.

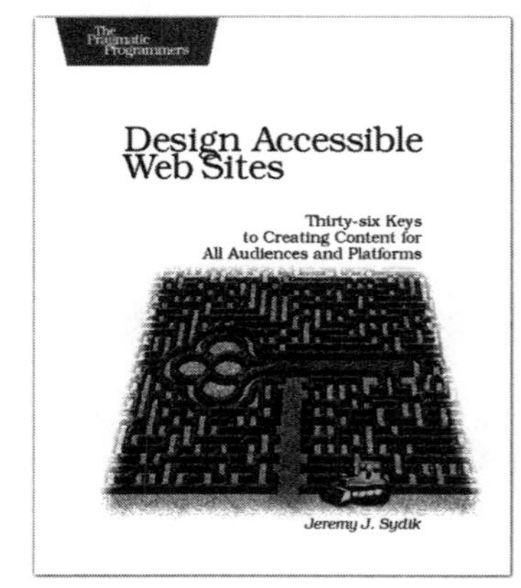

Design Accessible Web Sites: 36 Keys to Creating Content for All Audiences and Platforms
Jeremy Sydik
(304 pages) ISBN: 978-1-9343560-2-9. $34.95
http://pragprog.com/titles/jsaccess

Getting It Done

Start with the habits of an agile developer and use the team practices of successful agile teams, and your project will fly over the finish line.

Practices of an Agile Developer

Agility is all about using feedback to respond to change. Learn how to • apply the principles of agility throughout the software development process • establish and maintain an agile working environment • deliver what users really want • use personal agile techniques for better coding and debugging • use effective collaborative techniques for better teamwork • move to an agile approach

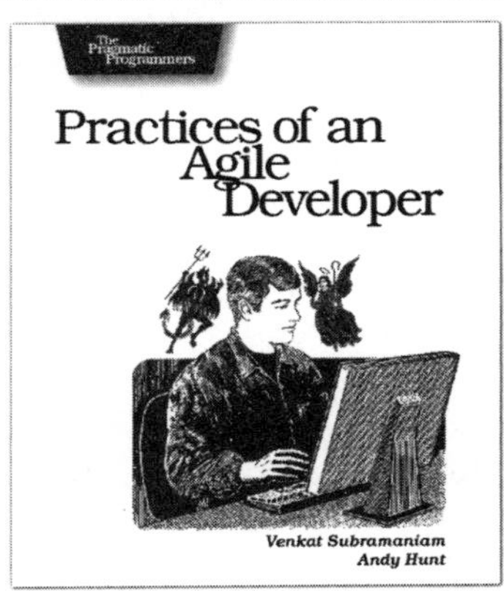

Practices of an Agile Developer: Working in the Real World
Venkat Subramaniam and Andy Hunt
(189 pages) ISBN: 0-9745140-8-X. $29.95
http://pragprog.com/titles/pad

Ship It!

Page after page of solid advice, all tried and tested in the real world. This book offers a collection of tips that show you what tools a successful team has to use, and how to use them well. You'll get quick, easy-to-follow advice on modern techniques and when they should be applied. **You need this book if:** • you're frustrated at lack of progress on your project. • you want to make yourself and your team more valuable. • you've looked at methodologies such as Extreme Programming (XP) and felt they were too, well, extreme. • you've looked at the Rational Unified Process (RUP) or CMM/I methods and cringed at the learning curve and costs. • **you need to get software out the door without excuses.**

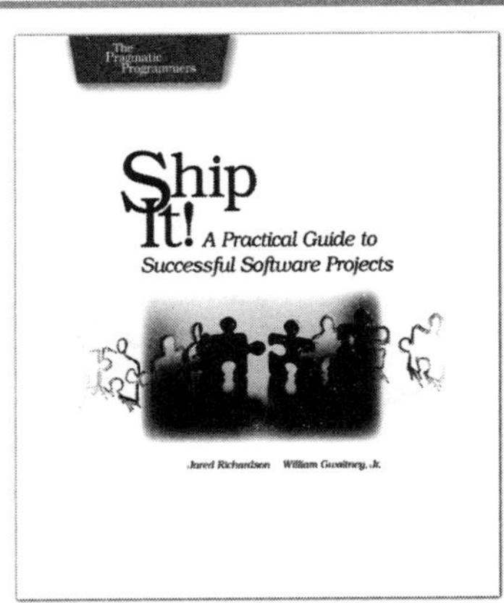

Ship It! A Practical Guide to Successful Software Projects
Jared Richardson and Will Gwaltney
(200 pages) ISBN: 0-9745140-4-7. $29.95
http://pragprog.com/titles/prj

It All Starts Here

If you're programming in Ruby, you need the PickAxe Book: the definitive reference to the Ruby Programming language, now in the revised 3rd Edition for Ruby 1.9.

Programming Ruby 1.9 (The Pickaxe for 1.9)

The Pickaxe book, named for the tool on the cover, is the definitive reference to this highly-regarded language.

• Up-to-date and expanded for Ruby version 1.9 • Complete documentation of all the built-in classes, modules, and methods • Complete descriptions of all standard libraries • Learn more about Ruby's web tools, unit testing, and programming philosophy

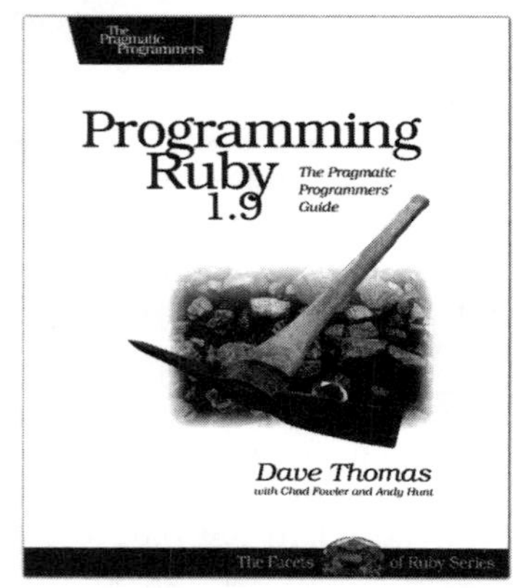

Programming Ruby 1.9: The Pragmatic Programmer's Guide for Ruby 1.9
Dave Thomas with Chad Fowler and Andy Hunt
(900 pages) ISBN: 978-1-9343560-8-1. $49.95
http://pragprog.com/titles/ruby3

Agile Web Development with Rails

Rails is a full-stack, open-source web framework, with integrated support for unit, functional, and integration testing. It enforces good design principles, consistency of code across your team (and across your organization), and proper release management. This is the newly updated Second Edition, which goes beyond the Jolt-award winning first edition with new material on:

• Migrations • RJS templates • Respond_to • Integration Tests • Additional ActiveRecord features • Another year's worth of Rails best practices

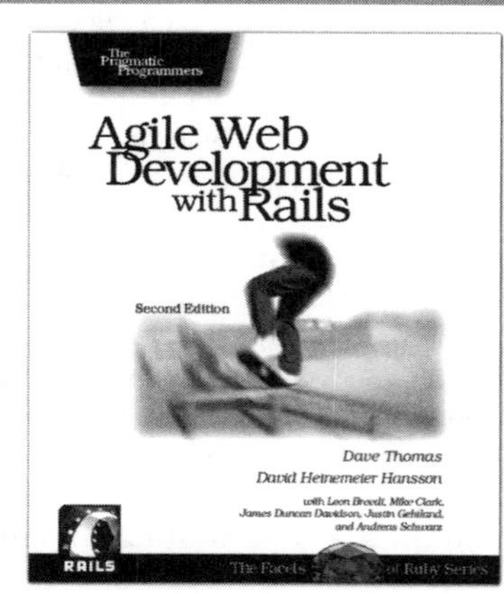

Agile Web Development with Rails: Second Edition
Dave Thomas and David Heinemeier Hansson with Leon Breedt, Mike Clark, James Duncan Davidson, Justin Gehtland, and Andreas Schwarz
(750 pages) ISBN: 0-9776166-3-0. $39.95
http://pragprog.com/titles/rails2

Stuff You Need to Know

Learn the best ways to use your own brain and the best ways to use Ubuntu Linux. Either way, this is stuff you need to know.

Pragmatic Thinking and Learning

Software development happens in your head. Not in an editor, IDE, or design tool. In this book by Pragmatic Programmer Andy Hunt, you'll learn how our brains are wired, and how to take advantage of your brain's architecture. You'll master new tricks and tips to learn more, faster, and retain more of what you learn.

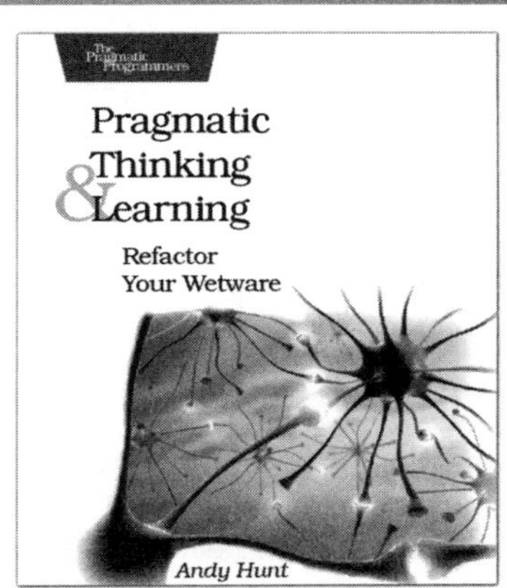

• Use the Dreyfus Model of Skill Acquisition to become more expert • Leverage the architecture of the brain to strengthen different thinking modes
• Avoid common "known bugs" in your mind
• Learn more deliberately and more effectively
• Manage knowledge more efficiently

Pragmatic Thinking and Learning: Refactor your Wetware
Andy Hunt
(288 pages) ISBN: 978-1-9343560-5-0. $34.95
http://pragprog.com/titles/ahptl

Ubuntu Kung Fu

Award-winning Linux author Keir Thomas gets down and dirty with Ubuntu to provide over 300 concise tips that enhance productivity, avoid annoyances, and simply get the most from Ubuntu. You'll find many unique tips here that can't be found anywhere else.

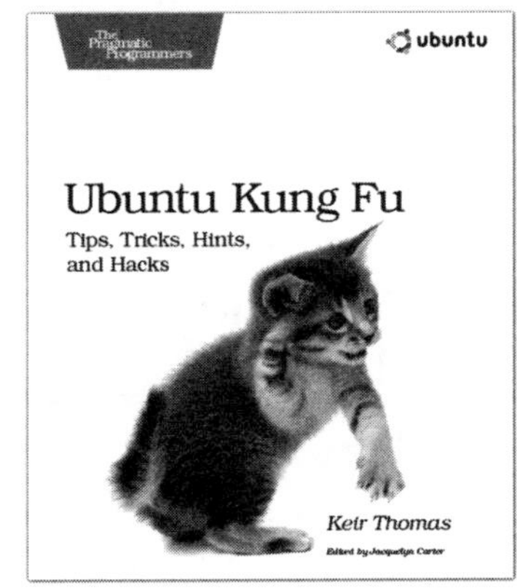

You'll also get a crash course in Ubuntu's flavor of system administration. Whether you're new to Linux or an old hand, you'll find tips to make your day easier.

This is the Linux book for the rest of us.

Ubuntu Kung Fu: Tips, Tricks, Hints, and Hacks
Keir Thomas
(400 pages) ISBN: 978-1-9343562-2-7. $34.95
http://pragprog.com/titles/ktuk

The Pragmatic Bookshelf

The Pragmatic Bookshelf features books written by developers for developers. The titles continue the well-known Pragmatic Programmer style and continue to garner awards and rave reviews. As development gets more and more difficult, the Pragmatic Programmers will be there with more titles and products to help you stay on top of your game.

Visit Us Online

Pragmatic Version Control Using Git's Home Page
http://pragprog.com/titles/tsgit
Source code from this book, errata, and other resources. Come give us feedback, too!

Register for Updates
http://pragprog.com/updates
Be notified when updates and new books become available.

Join the Community
http://pragprog.com/community
Read our weblogs, join our online discussions, participate in our mailing list, interact with our wiki, and benefit from the experience of other Pragmatic Programmers.

New and Noteworthy
http://pragprog.com/news
Check out the latest pragmatic developments in the news.

Save on the PDF

Save on the PDF version of this book. Owning the paper version of this book entitles you to purchase the PDF version at a terrific discount. The PDF is great for carrying around on your laptop. It's hyperlinked, has color, and is fully searchable.

Buy it now at pragprog.com/coupon.

Contact Us

Phone Orders:	1-800-699-PROG (+1 919 847 3884)
Online Orders:	www.pragprog.com/catalog
Customer Service:	orders@pragprog.com
Non-English Versions:	translations@pragprog.com
Pragmatic Teaching:	academic@pragprog.com
Author Proposals:	proposals@pragprog.com